Emma Wright is a speaker, writer and body-confidence parenting coach who is redefining the meaning of 'healthy' in a weight-obsessed world. As an eating disorder survivor and a parent, she wanted her kids to relate to their bodies in a way that she didn't. Diving into the research, she discovered the surprising truth about weight and unrestricted diets, and through her speaking events and courses, she has coached hundreds of parents in Aotearoa and around the world to nurture their kids towards healthier relationships with food and their bodies. She offers events and resources under the name Raising Body-Confident Kids.

Body-Confident

A guide to raising happy eaters

EMMA WRIGHT

HarperCollins*Publishers*

HarperCollins*Publishers*
Australia • Brazil • Canada • France • Germany • Holland • India
Italy • Japan • Mexico • New Zealand • Poland • Spain • Sweden
Switzerland • United Kingdom • United States of America

First published in 2024
by HarperCollins*Publishers* (New Zealand) Limited
Unit D1, 63 Apollo Drive, Rosedale, Auckland 0632, New Zealand
harpercollins.co.nz

A catalogue record for this book is available from the National Library of New Zealand

ISBN 978 1 7755 4242 1 (pbk)
ISBN 978 1 7754 9273 3 (ebook)
ISBX 978 1 4607 3548 0 (audiobook)

Cover design by Michelle Zaiter, HarperCollins Design Studio
Cover images by istockphoto.com
Typeset in Minion Pro Regular by Kirby Jones
Author photograph by Leigh Jeffery
Printed and bound in Australia by McPherson's Printing Group

CONTENTS

Introduction 1

SECTION ONE Food

Chapter 1: Why kids behave around food like they do 21
Chapter 2: How our kids get their needs met 33
Chapter 3: From food battles to empowerment and calm 45
Chapter 4: New tools for your new role 65

SECTION TWO Fat

Chapter 5: A short history of the body mass index 87
Chapter 6: Correlation vs causation 101
Chapter 7: A new perspective on health and weight 114
Chapter 8: Why are we so bothered by fat? 133
Chapter 9: Environment matters 155

SECTION THREE Fear

Chapter 10: Effective communication with your child 183
Chapter 11: When eating gets disordered 204
Chapter 12: Bodies and sex 212
Chapter 13: Sleep 227
Chapter 14: Social media and device competence 235

Final words 257

Acknowledgements 267
References and endnotes 269
Resources and helpful links 280

Author's note

All names and identifying characteristics of the parents who agreed to share their stories for this book have been changed. Their children's names, ages and identifying characteristics have also been changed. If a story within this book reflects your personal story, it is by coincidence. I wish to thank everyone who agreed to participate so that other parents can learn from their challenges and successes.

This book only provides general information regarding physical and mental wellbeing and does not take account of individual circumstances. This book is not in any way a substitute for medical advice or counselling. Always consult with a qualified medical practitioner or counsellor to address your child's specific physical and mental needs or if you suspect your child has an eating disorder. The author and publisher do not accept any liability for any injury, loss or damage that may arise from reliance on the information contained in this book.

Introduction

It started with a simple question to her daughter and ended in a conversation Rose felt entirely unprepared for. The school term was about to begin, so Rose asked ten-year-old Mia if she wanted to be signed up for swimming once or twice a week.

'I'm not swimming anymore, Mum,' came Mia's defiant reply.

'Why not, darling?'

'My legs are too fat to wear togs, and everyone thinks I'm ugly.'

Rose's blood ran cold. In truth, she'd rather have heard Mia say almost anything than 'I'm fat'. How was she supposed to handle this conversation without making things infinitely worse?

From the get-go, Rose had been committed to doing all the right things when it came to her daughter's health and wellbeing. But instead of seeing freedom and happiness in her ten-year-old, she had been watching helplessly as Mia began to wear baggy clothes and avoid social situations. Now Mia had said it out loud: she hated her fat legs.

Rose had been worried for a while, but whenever she told Mia she was gorgeous and not fat and that she shouldn't worry, she was met with eye rolls and different iterations of 'you don't understand'. It frightened Rose. She wanted Mia to be healthy (of course!), but she didn't want her to have body image issues either. Lying awake at night, Rose worried about what to say and do, trying to figure out how to stop what felt like a runaway train.

Rose knew the pain of food and body struggles only too well. She wasn't as slim as she'd have liked to be. In fact, she had struggled with her body her entire life, and it'd only got worse since her children were born. She didn't want that for them. Not at all. She had always believed that if she worked hard to get her kids into healthy habits, by teaching them what was good to eat and what wasn't, they would grow up to be slim and fit, and wouldn't hate their bodies like she did. So she fed them veggies at most meals, warned them of the dangers of being fat, and made sure they knew good foods from bad.

Sound familiar? You may have met people like Rose with children like Mia, but in truth, they are fictional characters, created from the stories I hear every day from parents caught in the triumvirate of getting their child to eat right, ensuring they don't put on too much weight and encouraging them to feel at home in their body.

I know Rose and Mia's story intimately, not just from the parents I work with, but because I have lived it. I suffered from an eating disorder when I was younger.

Like so many women, the pain of not liking my body had consumed a large part of my life. I knew the desperation of trying again and again to eat the right way so that I could finally become slim and stop worrying.

The decision to 'start Monday' made over and over again. The anguish of seeing myself in the mirror and feeling nothing but disgust. The programmes and supplements I'd paid good money for and food groups I'd cut out in the desperate hope that *this* would be the thing. The belief that if I could only drop a couple of dress sizes, I'd be liked, accepted, successful and admired, and life would be easier. It drove me to exercise until there was no room for much else in my life. Guilt and shame visited and overstayed every time I didn't 'put in the training' or eat in a way I'd promised myself I would.

Try as I might to get thoughts of food and weight out of my head, they persisted, making me feel out of control, embarrassed and like I was fundamentally broken. Yet from conversations with friends over the years, I knew that I wasn't the only one who had these experiences – even if it often felt that way.

To say I didn't want any of that for my children was an understatement. After giving birth to them, soaked through with love and wonder and marvelling at each precious new face, I promised, 'I will not let you feel the same way about your body and food as I have. Not on my watch.'

The problem was that when my children were born, in the mid-2000s, I believed everything Rose believed. The key to a body-confident child was healthy habits taught young, with a generous side of praise for their gorgeousness. There was no question that healthy food would be a cornerstone of my parenting, and I thought that if I could ensure healthy eating habits were ingrained in my children as young as possible, they'd be set for life. If I did this, I mistakenly believed, it would inoculate them from the mental anguish I'd experienced in the pursuit of controlling what I ate and managing my body.

It wasn't just about ensuring they avoided the pain of not liking their bodies either. I was convinced they'd be healthier and happier if I could guarantee they wouldn't get fat. They'd feel accepted and respected and avoid the many health problems that I'd been led to believe visited only bigger folks. It would also pin me as a good parent.

Somewhere along the way, I'd internalised the idea that a child's weight was a mother's responsibility, and I took that responsibility seriously. I'd read the memos about 'healthy weight' and the 'obesity epidemic' and allowed them to influence my actions.

I may not have been able to articulate all that to you back then, or even admit to it, but in retrospect many of the things I did as a young parent were driven by those beliefs.

My children were still preschoolers when I noticed that simply providing healthy food didn't achieve the results I'd been told it would. My kids didn't like the nutrient-dense food I gave them, no matter how much time I spent chopping it into pleasing shapes, making star charts or introducing rewards. They'd either eat nothing, or they'd fuss, moan and beg, and then eat way beyond fullness in situations where I wasn't there to control them. Rather than happily bonding over shared meals, we battled. The most consistent outcome from my efforts was stress and anxiety for me and misery for them.

Thanks to my commitment to healthy, organic food, I bought as much as possible from the 'health' aisle and spent more money than we had budgeted for on healthy options. But at a preschool health check-up, a doctor suggested that 'perhaps it's time to make some healthy changes'. I wasn't asked what I was feeding my kids, or about my commitment to their health. Instead, the assumption was explicit – I must have been feeding them too much, or the wrong things.

Unfortunately, instead of realising the approach I was taking didn't work for them or me, I simply tried harder. I became more stringent about sweets and processed foods, what was good and what was bad, and what was acceptable to have at home. I believed I wasn't doing a good-enough job of providing the right foods in the right ways, and if I could just do what I was supposed to be doing *better*, it would all work out.

Looking around and swapping notes with other parents, I observed plenty of frustration similar to mine. I saw very little freedom or joy when it came to food and bodies. There were many serious, fearful discussions about sugar. Some parents resorted to sending their kids to parties with their own food; while some kids had life-threatening allergies that made this necessary, many parents did this with the vague notion of 'being healthier'. I heard other parents discussing how bad it was to send chips or yoghurt pottles or highly processed foods in lunch boxes, and, in outraged tones, how some people allowed their children to eat nothing but frankfurters. I heard a lot of judgement about how children were the size they were due to their parents' poor food choices. I'm embarrassed to admit that I dished out a fair share of judgement myself. I wish I could go back and apologise to every parent I thought was doing the wrong thing.

By the time my kids were at school, one thing I knew for sure was that feeding kids healthy food was certainly not as simple as 'if I serve it, they will eat it'. And it wasn't just me. It was becoming clear that many other parents were struggling, despite doing all the right things. The most heart-wrenching conversations were with parents whose values and approach were the same as mine, who said things like, 'I don't know what to do. Yesterday, Eden said she'd rather be thin than do well at school.' I knew these mothers didn't want their children to feel that way, just like I didn't. And yet here we were.

It dawned on me that our collective inability to 'instil healthy habits' wasn't the problem. Maybe the anxiety, battles and concerning behaviour that we were seeing and experiencing was actually the most common outcome of this 'healthy habits' approach.

We were doing our best, buying the most nutritious foods, getting as many veggies into our kids as we could, and reminding them that they were gorgeous. Still, it just wasn't generating the results we had been promised. Food remained a battleground, no matter how hard we tried to control what our kids were eating. They still wanted sugar, sweets and chips, and they didn't seem to be on track to feeling good in their bodies. I realised that trying to control what our kids ate and how big they got didn't lead to better health. All that effort to do the right thing wasn't instilling body confidence; it was stealing it.

With a sinking heart, I knew if I was going to raise my children to eat without overthinking or hating what they saw in the mirror – making good on my promise to them at birth – I would have to find another way. So I did the only thing I could think of to do. I decided to seek a scientific understanding of the topic. I'd written a master's thesis back in the 1990s, so I knew how to assess evidence to see if it was likely to be based on sound methodology or if it just sounded 'sciencey' and didn't actually tell us anything. I also knew when to ask questions from people with a higher level of research-methodology training than I had. The research surprised me. The extent of the data, for starters, was astonishing: we have almost 100 years of research on this topic. As I dived into it, I began to question everything we had been doing, and I quickly understood that we needed a whole new set of parenting tools that reached far beyond 'healthy food habits'.

I discovered that to raise a kid who is at home in their body and has freedom around food, we have to think about much more than food and weight. It became apparent that focusing on a child having a 'not fat' body is an unhelpful distraction. If 'not being fat' plays a large role in the body confidence we teach our children, feelings of anguish and failure are a more likely outcome than physical and psychological wellbeing. This means that if we focus on making our kids eat right and ensuring they don't put on too much weight, we are more likely to end up with the opposite of what we want for our kids. It can even usher them towards an eating disorder, regardless of their size – and no parent wants that.

Thankfully, I found that it is possible for a child's experience of food and their body to be completely different from their parent's. It doesn't matter how the child (or the parent) felt about their body and food in the past, or how they feel now.

There is research to suggest that children can become relaxed around food and comfortable in their own bodies, but – this surprised me the most – it is difficult to help them get there using conventional parenting tools or food rules.

It's hard to grow up feeling good about your body if you're not taught to trust and respect its size, shape and uniqueness, or your appetite, desires, hunger and fullness. And unfortunately (and this is one of the most critical points I discovered in the studies I found), it's also hard for any of us to feel good about our bodies without challenging some deeply entrenched and harmful beliefs about food and bodies.

This book will challenge much of what you've been told and disabuse you of a few 'that's just the way it is' beliefs. It might feel confronting. There were times when the research I read made me want to throw it across the room. Some of the messages were difficult to accept. Many studies debunked what my friends, family and broader culture believed to be accurate. I had to learn to be open-minded and to loosen my grip – and you will too.

I'll ask you what I asked myself: how well has the status quo served you thus far? How well do you think it will serve your child?

How often have you promised yourself that the health kick, bootcamp or lifestyle change will start Monday? Perhaps, like Rose and me, you

Instead of wanting my kids to be effortlessly slim, I wanted them to respect and care for their bodies, and to reject messages that told them their bodies were flawed.

can relate to making new year's resolutions that promise health but are really about managing weight. Unfortunately, the more I've learned, the more I've come to see that programmes that include a weight-loss goal (either explicit or implied) rarely lead to food freedom or feeling more than fleetingly good about our bodies; more often than not, they lead to anxiety, frustration and a sense of failure. Those things tend to work against our long-term health. Thankfully, you can help your child avoid that trap, and it doesn't have to be like that for you either.

The new approach I discovered to food and bodies and parenting isn't a better way to get your child to eat vegetables, and it doesn't promise anyone a certain body size or shape. Instead, it will ask you to set aside the rules you've been clinging to, and to embrace a new way of thinking. In doing so, a new way of parenting will emerge – one that asks you to stop trying to get your kid to eat right and not put on too much weight. It will allow you to see your child growing up secure in the knowledge that their body is inherently good and worthy of the best care possible, and that how they look isn't the most important thing about them.

As I implemented this new approach, my relationship with food began to change beyond recognition. I started to confront one of the most significant prices I'd paid for trying to fix my body by managing what I ate: the mental space I had given it over the years. When my food fixation disappeared, and I stopped thinking about my body so much, the mental space I was left with felt close to miraculous.

These new experiences made me want something very different for my kids. Instead of wanting them to be effortlessly slim, I wanted them to respect and care for their bodies, and to reject messages that told them their bodies were flawed. I wanted them to eat without overthinking, and to eat the same way whether I was in the room or not. I didn't want them to hate seeing their reflection or measure their worth by the size of their jeans.

I wanted them to believe that who they are as people is more important than how they look, and to know that if someone bullies them about their body then something is wrong with that person, not them. I wanted them to have resilience and grit, and to stand up for themselves in the face of adversity or peer pressure.

If we want these things for our children, we have to zig where our culture is zagging. And that's what this book invites you to do. It requires looking at parenting from a perspective that is broader than just nutrition. A theme you'll hear again and again in this book is that *it's our job to set our children up to learn for themselves, because ultimately it's their body, and it will work best when they are in charge of it.*

In a wider sense, this book is about more than just food and bodies. It's about putting our kids in the driver's seat of their own lives wherever we can.

To do that we need to understand what motivates our children's behaviour, to help them self-regulate sleep and screen-time, to teach them to fight for their body to be accepted and respected, even when – especially when – it does not align with culturally sanctioned measurements. We need to engage in difficult conversations so that they'll come back to us when they really need us, rather than think,

I could never tell my parents that! In other words, we need an entirely different approach to our children, one that goes beyond technical parenting tools and focuses instead on trusting our children so they can trust themselves.

Before diving in, please understand that this is indeed a parenting book. While I've reviewed scientific studies and hold a master's degree in social science (my thesis is called 'Playing With Beauty', and it examines how social expectations of appearance affect female athletic performance), this book is written from a parent's perspective. I'm not a dietician, nutritionist, psychologist or therapist. Most importantly, I'm not an eating disorder specialist. Eating disorders are serious and can develop quickly. If you have any reason to think you or your child has an eating disorder, it is vital that you seek professional help – see page 280 for resources. That said, if you or your child are dealing with an eating disorder, this book will be helpful for you when it comes to broader parenting issues regarding food, and in preventing unhelpful cultural messages from entering your home, dealing with social media and having hard conversations so they will listen.

As such, this book is primarily a parenting guide, outlining everything I've learned since first making a promise to my kids. At first, I shared this knowledge with close friends. But these discussions, initially confined to our living rooms, soon found a wider audience as I got invited to present at local then national schools, at which point it became a full-time occupation. Over the years, the same questions kept surfacing, and I realised the universal relevance of these issues.

This book is a culmination of that journey, a resource I've created to help parents navigate their challenges.

There is no one right way to parent. This book is more launching pad than route planner. You can tweak the ideas and suggestions to work for your family and your unique circumstances.

After discovering and implementing this new approach, I now have the tools to raise body-confident kids, as do the parents I have worked with. Many of them tell me that their children no longer sneak food, wage battles at the dinner table or say they hate their legs. These parent trust their kids to eat what's right for them in a way they had no idea they could. They report that their teens tell them when Tik-Tokers try to make them feel bad about their body and they now seek out influencers of all shapes and sizes. I get messages from relieved parents telling me their children understand that body-shaming and anti-fat bias are cultural problems that they can help to eliminate.

In learning how to cultivate body confidence in children, my relationship with food and my body improved well beyond what I had imagined possible. These days, I hardly ever think about what I eat, and I'm comfortable in my skin, knowing that who I am is far more important than the size of the container I get about in. Although there will always be more work to be done, I am aware that my body size comes with privileges, and that I am responsible for making the world a better place for all bodies, not just mine. I want you to have these tools too!

Let's go.

SECTION ONE

Food

When parents seek me out for help, it's almost always because they're worried about their child: worried about their size, what they are eating, how they are exercising, how they are feeling about themselves and the messages they are getting from society.

Andrea came to see me because her 12-year-old son, Sam, didn't want to take his shirt off at the beach with his friends. As she described what was happening, it became clear that Andrea was focusing on food to help make things better for Sam. She was doing her best to help him eat as healthily as possible, being very careful never to mention dieting or weight loss, and telling him he was handsome and awesome. She encouraged him to eat well so he could avoid being the kid who gets teased about his weight at school. Andrea knew that pain intimately and didn't want it for her child.

Like many parents, Andrea had internalised the message that what you eat is directly linked to your body size. So it wasn't surprising that she was doing her best to help Sam make what she felt were better choices. Maybe you've done that too. I certainly have.

When I talk about food with parents like Andrea, they often say that it's unclear why things aren't working because they are doing what they've been told they should. In Andrea's case, despite her efforts, Sam wasn't getting any more confident. He certainly wasn't more likely to swim with friends. In fact, if anything, he seemed more withdrawn and was getting sneakier about what he was eating.

So instead of beginning our session by figuring out strategies to help Sam become comfortable in a swimsuit around his friends, Andrea and I looked at how she approached food and eating in their home. That's because a parent's preconceived ideas about eating a certain way often get in the way of helping their kids feel better about their bodies.

Regardless of your specific worry about your child, the most useful way to start is by understanding the feeding relationship you have in your home. This is the foundation that will allow you to address your concerns.

In this section, we'll begin with a deep dive into what motivates your kids to eat (and what motivates them in general), so that you are working with their motivations, not against them. Next, you will learn how to set up food and feeding in your house in a way that will lead to your children eating without fixating on food, and eating the same way whether you're supervising them or not.

As you read, I'll ask you to pull yourself out of the details of what you are currently doing and look at what you would like to achieve in the feeding relationship. For example, do you want them to consistently do what you ask (that would make for very easy parenting, wouldn't it?), or do you want them to nourish themselves well and care for their bodies (that's a much more challenging parenting task, but a healthier one)?

In doing all this, I suggest you stop trying to do the impossible, which also happens to be the basis of most parenting advice regarding food: making your kids eat a certain way.

Instead, I will suggest that you learn how to *trust* your children to eat what is right for them, without having to *make* them do anything.

CHAPTER 1

Why kids behave around food like they do

It's impossible for me to know your exact concerns about your child. I also have no idea how you set up food and feeding routines in your home. Maybe food isn't a big deal. Maybe it's a nightmare. Regardless, understanding the motivations human beings have to eat (over and above the obvious, that we need it for survival) will give you pause to make some shifts. For you, a shift may be monumental or subtle. It all depends on your family and what you are currently doing.

Here's the rub. Most of the information you've heard about kids and health implies it's your job to make them eat a certain way. You'll have been advised to teach them to eat good food and avoid bad, limit fat and sugar, and use dessert as a reward for eating veggies. Maybe you've done all those things.

It’s about understanding why they are eating, so that we can create an environment in which they can learn to eat in a way that works best for their unique body.

As you're about to see, we can't actually make them eat anything, and when we try, things snag in ways we might not expect. But it's not quite as simple as just letting them eat whatever they want, whenever they want. It's about understanding why they are eating, so that we can create an environment in which they can learn to eat in a way that works best for their unique body.

So let's poke around a bit at the premise that we, the parents, can't make them eat anything. You might be thinking, *Actually, I can. I can set consequences, like no ice cream until they've finished their greens. I can put their Halloween lollies away and allow only one piece at a time. I can send them to birthday parties with their own food and explain that they shouldn't eat any food they haven't brought with them.*

It's true that by putting tight controls in place, you may be able to elicit short-term compliance. But what happens when you're not in the room? What happens when they have the money and the maturity to go to the shop and make decisions for themselves? Research shows that a child who has their diet largely controlled by their parents when growing up is likely to eat a less nutritious diet when older.

So when I say we can't make them eat a certain way, I mean that we can't make them eat a certain way *in the long run*. And even in the short run, we can't make them eat a certain way without manipulation, coercion and control, which isn't a proven method to make anyone do anything willingly or happily.

Ultimately, what goes in their mouth is up to them. When we understand that they have this ultimate control, we can start to see our job as the provider of food in a very different light. We start to see that it's *about helping our child figure out what works for them*, rather than getting them to comply with our rules. This approach starts by understanding the three reasons our kids eat.

The three reasons kids eat

Eating for physical/nutritional satisfaction

This is easy to understand, right? Your child is hungry or tired, or wants to eat because their body needs energy or nutrition. Their tummy rumbles, they have an empty feeling, they're craving food. Almost all health and wellbeing advice directed at parents makes it sound like physical or nutritional satisfaction is the only (or at least the most) important reason for eating. It's not, and problems arise when we fail to consider the other two reasons.

While the nutritional content of food is an important aspect of physical satisfaction, many nutritionists argue that getting *enough* trumps all. We have come to a point in time where we are so focused on what we should limit, avoid or cut out altogether, that we've forgotten the very basics of good nutrition. Human beings need *enough* food, otherwise they suffer. Not getting enough is uncomfortable, it makes us fixate on food, it drives up our hunger hormones and focuses our attention on food in a way that can feel obsessive and like we're 'addicted'. Sometimes just allowing your child to eat more of what they want (and often it's the white starchy stuff that we've been taught to fear) smooths out all sorts of eating and feeding problems. Kids stop sneaking food and fixating on it; they are calmer and they sleep better.

Eating for emotional satisfaction

Children sometimes eat to feel happy or calm, or for a sense of social connection to those around them. Hearing that kids eat for emotional reasons might make your heart sink. You might be thinking, *Emotional eating has been such an issue for me, I really don't want my kid to be an emotional eater!* The fear you have is valid and needs addressing. But before we do that, let's look at emotional eating from an important but often missed standpoint.

Emotional eating, as Isabel Foxen Duke from the Stop Fighting Food programme points out, is by and large a natural and healthy aspect of eating. Think about how human beings enjoy eating as part of social celebrations or family gatherings: for example, the delight we get from a shared birthday cake or going out for pizza with friends. This kind of social eating is a joyful, emotionally satisfying activity.

All human cultures have social eating routines and rituals. Eating together plays a vital role in helping us feel connected to one another, and emotional satisfaction is at its core. As you read this book, you'll come back again and again to the role that connection and belonging plays in your child's life, and how you can create an environment where their sense of connection and belonging is nurtured.

But what about eating to soothe emotions – that's not the same thing, is it? Many people eat to soothe feelings of anxiety, shame, frustration, sadness and fear. If you have ever seen the way a lollipop at the doctor's office can calm a child with remarkable efficacy, you've seen eating for emotional soothing at play.

There is a school of thought that says this kind of emotional soothing is ultimately bad for kids and that food shouldn't be used for such purposes. One fear is that children won't learn to care for themselves in a healthier manner. It's easy to find advice that suggests we should teach kids alternatives to eating if they're upset or emotionally triggered. Some wellness practitioners suggest bathing due to the powerful calming effect of water. Others propose naming emotions, mindful breathing, journalling (once your child is old enough to write) or spending time in nature.

Let it be said: these are fantastic ways to soothe emotions, and fabulous additions to your child's toolkit. I am a huge advocate for helping children become adults who can feel, express and handle their emotions. The problem arises when we think that eating should be *excluded* from acceptable emotionally soothing activities – or that if we eat to soothe, we should only eat 'healthy' snacks that have been prepped in advance. I've even seen emotional eating categorised as a truly dangerous way for children and teens to handle emotional stress, alongside drinking, vaping, having unsafe sex or doing drugs.

Helping our children handle their stress so they don't lean on potentially damaging activities is an idea I can get behind. Demonising emotional eating, however, I cannot.

Let me explain. When I was in recovery from my eating disorder, I had to learn to feel emotions *and* to embrace emotional eating. If a strong emotional desire to eat struck me at a time when I couldn't stop and attend to my stress (right before a work presentation, for example, or in the middle of getting the kids to bed), I discovered that eating the thing I desired in the moment would buy me time until I was free to journal or cry or scream or leave the job, or whatever it was that was at the heart of my strong emotional response.

Teaching a child body confidence is, at least in part, about helping your child be okay with the more difficult sensations of the human experience, like fear, shame, anxiety and dread. I believe there is a case for having a safe way to calm those emotions in the moment, until we have time to process those emotions later. Emotional eating can do that, and do it well.

If a child sneaks food, they may be responding to food restrictions. Sneaking, after all, is a great way to get the food their body needs (physical or nutritional satisfaction), but they may also be responding to a need to self-soothe. Unfortunately, when children sneak food or display uncontrolled behaviour in their eating, parents are often advised to restrict their children's food further. They are told to keep certain foods out of reach or to avoid bringing those foods into the house. Parents sometimes go as far as locking the fridge and pantry doors.

Tactics like these give rise to some pretty big questions. If eating can provide such a beautiful sense of connection and belonging, and if it can also provide a quick, safe way to self-soothe as part of a wider skill set for handling emotions, why is emotional eating cast in such a poor light? Why is it so deeply feared? Why are we advised it's so important to stop?

The short answer is that emotional eating can become binge eating, which is as unpleasant as it is harmful. The long answer reveals *why and how* emotional eating becomes binge eating, and this will be addressed in the section on fear, where we look at what happens when eating gets disordered.

Eating for agency satisfaction

The third reason kids eat is to exert control or agency over their lives. Remember, the basic premise of this section is that, as a parent, you cannot make your child eat anything (bar using force or manipulation). Indeed, eating is one of the few things most children have complete and ultimate control over.

If a child is not getting enough agency satisfaction over the foods they eat or, importantly, agency satisfaction in their day-to-day lives, they might eat as a means of gaining control over their world.

When I learned that I had less control over what my child ate than I thought, it was both terrifying and a huge relief. I loved that I could let go and not have that battle with them anymore. I was also terrified that they would eat nothing but chocolate and ice cream for the rest of their lives, and I didn't know what to do with that fear. If you're feeling the same way, rest assured these fears will be addressed later in this book.

If you are experiencing power struggles with your child around food, they are likely to be experiencing a lack of *agency satisfaction*. If so, the following chapters, where we look at setting up peaceful mealtimes and creating freedom and confidence, will be particularly helpful for you. Learning ways to provide agency satisfaction to your child in positive ways is going to be a game-changer.

If a child is not getting enough agency satisfaction over the foods they eat or, importantly, agency satisfaction in their day-to-day lives, they will eat as a means of gaining control over their world.

* * *

Before we get to practicalities, let me suggest the order in which you attend to your child's eating needs. *Agency satisfaction* is the first thing to address in the feeding relationship because it will create a strong foundation of perceived agency over what goes in their mouth, and reduces their urge to battle.

Then you can focus on *emotional satisfaction* by creating and allowing for eating experiences that are enjoyable and calm. This will help boost your child's sense of emotional wellbeing.

Once you've established those two things, it's time to gently steer your child toward nutritional choices that can improve *physical satisfaction.*

Suppose we shoot straight into physical satisfaction and set out to teach our children about nutrition before their agency or emotional needs are satisfied? In that case, our efforts are likely to end in fighting, sneaking or concerning interactions around food.

Understanding behaviour more holistically

Now that you understand the three reasons kids eat, it's going to be helpful to understand their behaviour more holistically. Why do they interrupt us, fight us, dig in their heels and refuse to do what we ask, even when it's obvious that what we are suggesting is a good idea? The short answer is that they do all of that because they are trying to get their needs met. The long answer starts by looking at what those needs are. I wish I'd known this stuff right from the get-go. But even though by the time I learned all of this my children were already at school, the difference it made in my parenting and their behaviour was dramatic.

I think our culture has done a great disservice to modern parents by making everything the parents' problem, instead of asking parents to support their kids to figure out their own problems. It's a subtle but important shift from 'I have to do this for them' to 'How can I help them do this themselves?'

When we elevate the perceived power of the parents as the ones who can make their children behave, eat well and be healthy, two unfortunate things happen. Parents can feel overwhelmed and ashamed when their kids don't turn out in the way they are led to believe they will, and kids don't get to experience their own sense of responsibility and power.

When kids don't need to tackle their own problems, a very different kind of problem is created. Instead of getting busy being creative and making use of their power in favourable ways, they get busy fighting us, being annoying and displaying all sorts of concerning behaviour. When it comes to their health, this misplaced understanding of who is responsible for what can lead to some scary issues, and more often than not, we don't see them coming.

So how do we go about giving them more responsibility? A good place to start is to understand some basic tenets of Adlerian psychology. It is grounded in the belief that behaviour is goal-oriented, and that humans behave in ways that help them get their needs met.

Alfred Adler was an Austrian medical doctor and psychotherapist, who argued in the 1920s that children have two primary goals: to belong and to feel significant. What he meant by this is that it's necessary for kids to feel connected to and respected by those around them, and to feel that their community wants them to be a part of it.

Humans are social creatures, and we all have a basic need to know how and where we fit into the social groups around us. In the previous chapter, we looked at how sharing a meal helps us meet one of our most basic human needs: a sense of belonging. For children, this means feeling emotionally connected to their parents and peers, and secure about how they fit within the world around them. If we ignore the importance of this, our children will make mealtimes as unpleasant for us as it is for them. It's difficult to feel like you belong and are welcome when you have someone observing your every move, offering instructions about what you are doing and getting visibly upset or angry when you do it wrong.

In addition to belonging, children need to feel significant. They want to feel valued and capable and that their contributions make a difference.

In the next chapter, we'll look at how you can start the process of helping your child meet these goals of belonging and significance in ways that lead to body confidence, resilience and self-belief.

CHAPTER 2

How our kids get their needs met

If a child has two main goals – to feel a sense of belonging and to feel significant – they have two main ways to get those needs met: power and attention.

Amy McCready from Positive Parenting Solutions, a leading parenting education programme, explains this beautifully on her website. She asks us to imagine that our children walk around with two big metaphorical buckets out in front of them. One is an attention bucket and one is a power bucket. Our children's behaviour, by and large, is driven by their quest to fill those buckets.

The good news is that children are naturally equipped to fill their own buckets. We don't have to worry about whether they will get enough attention or power; they are capable of achieving that themselves. The challenge arises when they seek to fulfil these needs in ways that can be disruptive or distressing to others and themselves.

Let's think about their need for attention. You know when you're engrossed in an activity and your child tries insistently to get your attention? If they're young, they might cling to you or climb on you. If they're a bit older, they might interrupt you or start arguing with you for what seems like no reason whatsoever. This behaviour is filling their attention bucket in the most effective, or only, way they know how.

Seen from this perspective, a child isn't behaving badly when they are demanding our attention. They are actually doing something pretty cool: getting their needs met by ensuring they get our attention. Throughout this book, you'll learn how to address their attention needs in a manner more beneficial and enjoyable to you both.

Now think about their need for power. Kids fill their power buckets through contribution and agency; that is, by having the opportunity to make decisions and participate actively in their own lives. This boosts their self-confidence and generates a sense of significance and purpose.

As parents, a child's need for power is critical to consider because kids have limited control over their lives compared to adults. Parents make almost all major decisions for a child; where they live and go to school, what foods are in the house, when bedtime is – the list goes on.

In situations where children aren't allowed to exert power appropriate to their needs, they may act out, become defiant and oppose our decisions. They'll battle with us, refuse our requests and do things that seem totally against their self-interest. They don't behave this way to be intentionally naughty. They do it to get their significance needs met by filling up that power bucket.

Once we know this, we can give our child as many appropriate ways as feasible to exert their independence. We can get them to plan meals, choose where to sit at the table and what food to put on their plate, decide what to wear and what haircut to have. As they mature, we can offload as much control over their lives as we can. Could they decide on the layout of the sitting room? Or decide how the family spends the day once a month? You can be as creative as you like with this and you can also ask your child to contribute ideas.

Once you recognise their need for power, you'll start to notice opportunities where you can cease making decisions for them and give them the independence to decide for themselves. Some parenting experts suggest we should seldom do something for a child that they can do for themselves. I think this is great advice.

How do children figure out what they are valued for?

So far you've learned the two ways that kids derive their sense of significance and belonging: through attention and power. Now we are going to look more closely at what happens when those power and attention needs are met in mostly inappropriate ways, and when they're met in mostly appropriate ways. The way our kids get their needs met has a huge influence on how they view themselves and how they decide what it is they are valued for as human beings.

Let's start with the overarching premise at play here. Kids form their self-beliefs based on what they think are the most important aspects of themselves, or what they are valued for.

Remember how I said that regardless of what we do, our kids will get their power and attention needs met? In a similar way, they will form a sense of value. It's a given. We don't have to worry about *whether* they will develop this sense, but we can have an impact on *what* they believe is valuable about themselves.

Building on this, a child will develop two types of value: internal and external. Internal value stems from within; it encompasses qualities like self-respect, inner strength and self-belief. An example of internal value is the self-worth a child feels when they overcome a challenge or learn a new skill, independent of external validation. On the other hand, external value is the approval or judgement they get from others; for example, praise or comments on physical appearance or material possessions.

So what? Why does it matter if we are valued for external attributes, instead of who we are inside? Is there really anything wrong with being appreciated and respected for external things?

There is nothing intrinsically wrong with external values like looks, status and achievements, and indeed all human beings will have a mixture of internal and external value. The problem with having our value hooked mainly to the external is that ultimately we don't have control over those things and, plus, they're always changing.

Our appearance changes as we age. An economic downturn might lead to a job loss. Our achievements will fade into the past.

Our internal values, however, remain ours. We can always choose kindness, consideration and love. We can contribute ideas. We can be creative and solve problems. We can always choose to practise bravery, even if the end result isn't within our control.

In his book *Lost Connections*, Johann Hari points out that when a person believes their worth hinges on external factors, their mental health is more likely to suffer and they will be more susceptible to body-confidence issues. That's why the tools and strategies in this book are designed to help boost your child's sense of internal value.

Whether you have toddlers or teens (or both!) at home, what you will learn will help you to cultivate your child's sense of belonging and significance in ways that can solidify their internal value.

Your need for control and power and why it matters

Just like our children, we need to feel a sense of significance and belonging, and have a sense of agency over our world, and we gain this via attention and power. Now that we have children, our world may feel more out of control than it used to. Many parents report feeling stressed, tired and in over their heads. Truth be told, I've occasionally wished my kids were grown and had flown the coop already, so I could stop feeling like a failure. In the early parenting years, if you had asked how in control of my world I felt, I'd have said 'not at all'.

One way to get your power needs met in a way that will feel good for you and your children is to start looking at your role as a parent

Instead of seeing the job in terms of getting your kids to act the way you want them to act – *eat your broccoli, put on a jacket, get some exercise!* – what would happen if you saw your role as helping them become capable adults?

from a different point of view. Instead of seeing the job in terms of getting your kids to act the way you want them to act – *eat your broccoli, put on a jacket, get some exercise!* – what would happen if you saw your role as helping them become capable adults? This is the first step in switching from the misguided notion that a parent's job is to solve their kids' problems to realising that parents can assist their kids to figure out the world *for themselves.*

In order to make this shift, I want you to do a thought experiment similar to the one parenting writer Michelle Icard shares in her book *Fourteen Talks by Age Fourteen*. Imagine you have the best boss in the world. They give you autonomy and treat every interaction like you are a capable person, worthy of respect. They understand that there is a learning curve to your job, that you'll sometimes make mistakes, and that you need their support to learn. They listen, accept your limitations and help you improve.

Now imagine a very different boss, who sees you as incompetent and in need of micromanaging. Perhaps they bark orders, get mad when you don't do the job their way, shout louder if you're not behaving how they'd like, get frustrated when you make mistakes, and forget you aren't as experienced as they are.

When we think about those two bosses, it can be helpful to understand that the first boss gets their sense of agency and control from helping employees succeed in their work. When employees are failing, this boss helps them to upskill, communicates effectively and takes great pleasure in watching their employees grow. You could argue the boss in this situation gets their power from making sure the environment is conducive to employees getting their jobs done.

The boss who barks orders meets their need for power and control by getting people to do things their way.

Both are legitimate, but one certainly works better for everyone involved.

When you find yourself in a power battle with your child – when you're getting frustrated and wanting them to comply – it can help to remember that you need power too, and that you have a choice. You can keep filling your power bucket by overpowering your child, or you can press pause, take a moment and aim to get your power in a very different way, by controlling yourself and the environment instead of controlling your child.

Here's an example.

You've asked your children not to drop their gear by the front door a million times. Usually, you find yourself, once again, shouting down the hall, 'Come and get your stuff off the floor now! How many times do I have to ask you?' When your kids finally pick up their gear, you blast them about not listening and how they need to show respect.

But this time, as you're standing there feeling irritated at the pile of bags and jackets by the door, you think, *What would the great boss do?* In a similar situation, they'd realise their employees weren't handling the request and they would treat it as a learning opportunity. They'd talk to the employees after the fact, rather than in the heat of the moment.

If you were to use this strategy with your kids, you'd sit them down and say, 'Hey, I've noticed that I've asked you on more than one occasion to use the hooks to hang up your bags and jackets, not drop them on the floor. Having the hallway free and clear is important so we don't trip over stuff and can open and close the door easily. In future, if you leave stuff on the floor, I'm going to put it in the boot of my car. You'll find it there if you need it, but you won't have to if you hang it up in the first place.'

Can you see how this approach will meet your power needs while giving respect and agency to your kids? They can choose to leave their things on the floor or not, but they have to deal with the hassle of going out to the car to get them if they do so.

The great thing about being a good boss is that you can start immediately. The next time you notice yourself battling with your child or feeling the need to make them comply, you can pause and remind yourself that it is possible to empower them and yourself to behave in ways that work well for everyone.

* * *

Now that you have insight into the roles of belonging and significance, attention and power, and internal and external value in your child's world, I'm going to share the first of many tools that will give your kids the attention and power they need while helping to solidify their sense of internal value. I call it Power Time, and it's a foundational tool for raising body-confident kids.

Power Time

Power Time is the practice of dedicating one-on-one time with your child and giving them your full attention while doing whatever they choose. Power Time gives you a chance to step away from being the boss and handing the reins over to your child. Don't forget, kids spell love 'T.I.M.E.', so when you give your kids Power Time they will experience being loved.

You may have heard this concept echoed in other parenting books, as numerous studies have shown that Power Time has proven to have measurable benefits for kids. Amy McCready from Positive Parenting Solutions, for example, calls it 'Mind, Body and Soul Time'. I love her terminology because it reminds us to give our mind, body and soul to our kids every day. I've noticed many kids, on the other hand, relate better to the term Power Time because they like the notion of having the power. Ultimately, it doesn't matter what you call it; the important thing is to make a habit of doing it.

Time spent one-on-one means giving your undiluted attention to each of your children individually, without competition from siblings. Your child drives the agenda, and your duty is to attentively engage. A common pitfall is distractions – whether it's checking your phone or zoning out. If you notice yourself getting distracted, bring your attention back. It's not easy to remain focused, I know, but the more you can manage, the bigger the rewards.

So, what kinds of activities qualify for Power Time? For younger children to tweens, it's ideally something that doesn't involve screens, driving or spending money. It can be as simple as role-playing farm animals: if they want to crawl around mooing, go for it. Using a timer can be beneficial, marking the session's start and end.

For teenagers, you might consider relaxing these guidelines. It could mean playing a video game or going shopping, as long as they are in charge and have your undivided attention.

Afterwards, tell them you loved your time together; this will reinforce your child's sense of belonging and internal value.

Power Time is not just a fun activity but an investment in your child's emotional wellbeing. It nurtures their sense of belonging, satisfies their attention needs and boosts their intrinsic value - all of which are vital components in building body confidence.

Consistency is key. Ideally, your child will get Power Time for ten minutes at the same time every day with each parent. Of course, that might not be possible. You might have three kids or work shifts or have health issues that don't allow for this kind of routine, but there are still many ways to make Power Time work.

If it's more realistic to give each child ten minutes twice a week, begin with that. Tell your kids when it's scheduled and that it's important to you.

A word of caution: don't put off Power Time by waiting until you have enough time. Chances are you won't. As we get busier, our kids' need for belonging and significance and to feel valued for who they are on the inside remains. As Amy McCready reminds us, we can spend time with our children in Power Time or we can spend time with them in power battles.

You might be thinking, *Yeah, but, seriously, how do I jam it into my life?* Well, you do exactly that: you jam it in. You are not going to miraculously find extra time, so please don't wait. Make a start and see what happens.

Now that you understand your child's need for belonging and significance, and the impact these things have on cultivating their sense of internal value, it's time to look at how all this relates to feeding them.

CHAPTER 3

From food battles to empowerment and calm

Susan came to me for help because she'd caught her eight-year-old son, Kaden, emptying his lunchbox into a neighbour's bin on the way to school. Not only that, but he was sneaking into the kitchen and filling his pockets with off-limits foods like chips and chocolate, and eating them while hiding in his room.

I asked Susan how she saw her role as a parent when it came to Kaden's eating habits. She said, 'Well, I need to ensure he eats well at each meal. I want him to know what is healthy and unhealthy. If he doesn't eat a balanced diet, that's on me.'

Let's think about that for a moment. In the last chapter, we learned that, ultimately, our kids decide how they act, and this includes what kinds of food they eat – and how much. And truly, that's a good thing.

Our role as parents isn't to make our kids eat what we want them to eat at each meal. Instead, it is to empower our kids to become competent eaters.

For Susan, that meant shifting her focus from trying to 'make him eat well' or stressing about short-term wins – *Has he eaten enough greens today?* – to a long-term goal – *Can he nourish himself well?*

I want to widen your view of your job description when it comes to feeding your kids, so you can see the whole iceberg and get a different perspective.

So, what is a competent eater? In my mind, it is someone who:

- has a positive and enjoyable relationship with food,
- eats the same way whether someone else is observing them or not,
- and knows how to nourish themselves well.

In other words, competent eating isn't about eating a balanced diet or eating the right things and avoiding the wrong things. A competent eater is a person who has the skills to consistently satisfy their three eating needs (agency satisfaction, emotional satisfaction and physical/nutritional satisfaction) in a way that works for them.

Notice how this definition doesn't mention health or weight, or particular kinds or amounts of food?

At this point, you may be wondering, *Don't I have to make sure they get enough fruit and veggies? We all know that eating fruits and veggies is good for them, but if I don't make them eat them, they'll never eat them.* I'm not disputing that eating fruits and vegetables is good for kids' health; it absolutely is. I'm not saying that you can't encourage the eating of them; you can. I'm suggesting that if they come to eat fruits and vegetables in their own time, without feeling pressured or forced into it, they are more likely to turn into lifelong fruit and veggie eaters. If you try to 'make' them, the opposite may end up happening.

As parents, we will do well to shift our role from figuring out how to get our kids to eat according to our expectations or desires to creating an environment where they are free to explore what makes their body feel best.

Indeed, this plays out in the research. Kids who learn to eat with competence are more likely to become adults who have a nutritionally diverse and balanced diet, and more positive quality-of-life indicators. Research from the Ellyn Satter Institute has shown that eating competence leads to better health outcomes in later life, regardless of your size, shape or weight. This research surprised me, but it also gave me the confidence to hand the reins of power to my children when it comes to what goes into their bodies.

Now that you know your job isn't to micro-manage each meal but to create an environment where your child can figure out what works for their body, let's look at how you can make this happen.

Dividing up responsibilities

A great starting point for creating a competent eating environment is to look at who is responsible for what at mealtimes. Ellyn Satter suggests dividing the responsibilities within the feeding relationship between you and your child and making sure everyone is clear on that division.

Up to the tween years, the parent has four distinct responsibilities:

1. Provide the food.
2. Create a calm environment to eat in: set mealtime rules and boundaries, and help keep the table an enjoyable place to be.
3. Choose what will be available to eat at each meal: meal plan and decide what foods the kids can choose from, being mindful of expanding their palates while providing enough that feels familiar and comfortable.
4. Set the times of day meals are eaten: offer kids plenty of opportunities to eat and let them know when the next opportunity is coming.

Now, let's look at your child's responsibilities. They have two:

1. Decide what to eat from what's on offer.
2. Decide how much to eat from what's on offer.

I encourage you to give your child full responsibility for what and how much they eat. I know this may sound alarming. As I said previously, I initially thought this meant my kids would eat nothing but chocolate and ice cream forever. You'll be pleased to know that didn't happen in my family, and it won't be the case in yours either. Plus, you do not need to make chocolate and ice cream available at every meal. The food on offer is still your responsibility.

Remember, children who are allowed to eat as much as they like of what's on offer end up with better long-term health outcomes – including eating a more nutritious diet – than kids who are tightly managed and controlled.

Before we dive into the nitty-gritty of allocating these new responsibilities, I want to touch on how this approach will be different once your kids become teenagers.

Once your child is a tween and beyond, you have less control over the food your child has access to and when they can eat, so you'll need to adjust the responsibilities as they grow. You will no longer be the only one providing the food. Your child will begin buying food for themselves and making choices about what they eat that you have no control over. Leaning into these changes is your responsibility. You can still have family mealtimes and expect your children to adhere to the rules, but you may find that dictating what can and can't be eaten between meals triggers a power struggle rather than helping your child feel comfortable around food.

In the resources section at the end of this book, you'll find a link to an interview with Evelyn Tribole, the original Intuitive Eating pro, who has many tips for teaching your tweens and teens to become competent eaters. The key is to start with trust, allow them to take full charge of their bodies, and continue to expect respectful behaviour at mealtimes without attempting to 'fix' or control what they are eating.

Raising competent eaters: the basics

Now that we've established that it's important to let kids take control of their eating satisfaction, let's look at how we can foster eating competence in our kids.

I get how exhausting it can be when the dining table becomes a battleground. It is sadly common for families to dread mealtimes, for fights to break out and for parents to feel helpless and overwhelmed. So let's get you armed with some tools that will put paid to unpleasant mealtimes.

1. *Create an eating routine.* Think about your children needing three meals plus two snacks a day. This isn't a hard-and-fast rule; your family might work better with three meals and three snacks. The point is to create a routine that remains reasonably consistent and helps your child understand that they are safe to feel hungry because a meal is always coming soon.
2. *Give as much autonomy as you can to your child.* Put the dishes in the middle of the table and allow your child to serve themselves. Tell them they are allowed as much or as little as they like of each dish, with the caveat that they only take their allocated portion of a limited dish; one steak each, for example. Give each child a turn to choose where everyone sits, or say the prayer if you do that, or choose which plates get used. If it means that every so often you eat dinner out of a bowl when a plate would be

better, allow it to happen. Take a minute now to jot down ideas about how you can offer your child more control at mealtimes.

3. *Encourage them by talking about who they are, not what they are eating.* Refrain from commenting on the food choices your child makes and instead ask them about their day or talk about an idea or an upcoming event. Here are some ways you can encourage your child during meals: 'It's so lovely to eat with you. What do you think about the table setting? What was the best part of your day?'
4. *Drop rewards.* Making dessert conditional on a child eating vegetables or rewarding healthy eating using a star chart sends the message that you don't think your child is capable of eating vegetables without an incentive. It also distracts your child from their own internal hunger, fullness and enjoyment cues, and makes them focus on an external reward.
5. *Avoid binary labels.* Dividing food into good and bad, healthy and unhealthy, fattening and slimming can be confusing and make kids anxious about what they eat.
6. *Avoid connecting food or eating to body size.* There is no scientific evidence that any one food can change someone's body weight in the long run. There are no foods that only bigger-bodied people eat and no foods that only smaller-bodied people eat. Linking

foods to body size adds to weight stigma and anxiety around food.

7. *Go slowly.* If your child has a limited palate and you want to expand it, introduce new dishes slowly.
8. *Keep the dishes separate.* If possible, keep the pasta separate from the sauce. Giving your child the opportunity to assemble their own dish is another way to get their power needs met. It also helps kids who struggle with foods that are touching each other or mixed together.
9. *Insist on manners and table etiquette.* Teaching your child to behave appropriately at the dinner table is a great way for them to boost their sense of importance. It shows that you believe they can do it, and your expectations of them will boost their sense of internal value.
10. *Close the kitchen between meals.* This can be a great way to shut down begging for snacks and grazing. However, if your child has been sneaking food, you should allow plenty of instances to satisfy their hunger for previously off-limit foods, otherwise closing the kitchen will only make the sneaking worse. For examples of traps to avoid, see point three in the breakout box on page 55.

If you have a particularly selective or picky eater and these strategies are not helping, I recommend you get outside help. You'll find suggestions in the resources section on page 281.

In many homes, parents find themselves playing the role of short-order cook to cater to the varying meal preferences of their children. If that's you, let your children know in advance that you won't be doing that anymore. Instead, you'll be preparing a single meal for everyone. Serve the meal family-style with dishes in the centre of the table so everyone can help themselves. They are free to have as much or as little as they desire. Assure them that you won't comment on their food choices. However, everyone should wait until all are seated before starting and practise good table manners. Always include at least one universally liked dish. It's okay if, occasionally, a child opts to eat just one item or prepares something simple for themselves. As you begin to introduce more adventurous dishes, ensure familiar options are also available.

Many parents tell me they notice a difference within the first week of using these approaches. By fostering a welcoming environment at the table and giving everyone the right to choose what goes on their plates, everyone naturally becomes more present and has more fun. It might not happen overnight, but you may notice that before too long, your family has become more connected.

If your child is showing signs of sneaking food, or if you've been using rewards in the past, please don't worry about it. It's going to be okay. Offer yourself compassion; you were doing what you thought was best. Remember, regardless of how they're doing now, it is possible for your child to become a competent eater. It's never too late to redirect your children to their internal cues, and to shift your parenting style from restrictions and rewards to encouragement and empowerment.

Keep returning to the tools for keeping mealtimes fun and connected. Focus on giving your children appropriate ways to fill their power and attention buckets and help them tune into their hunger, fullness and satisfaction. As you do this, you'll see them start to trust their bodies and become competent eaters.

Three traps to avoid when teaching eating competence

1. *Short-order cooking.* It is not your job to customise meals for fussy eaters. Preparing separate dishes for each child suggests that you doubt their ability to expand their palates, which is disempowering for them. It also implies they can dictate your cooking choices, which is disempowering for you. This can easily become a power struggle instead of an actual feeding issue.
2. *Allowing kids to graze all day.* If a child constantly snacks, they may never experience genuine hunger. That can make it challenging for them to try new foods or eat a substantial meal. When we set meal times and inform our kids when the next meal will be, they can understand the sensation of hunger and feel confident that a meal

is on the horizon. That said, limiting access to food can be counterproductive for older children, especially if they can buy their own. For older, more independent kids, prioritise fixed mealtimes they should join, emphasising the importance of family time, conversation and using their manners.

3. *Limiting opportunities to learn.* If your child loves cookies, then every so often it can be helpful for them to have as many cookies as they want. This allows them to learn in a safe environment what a tummy full of cookies feels like. If your child is only ever allowed one cookie, then as soon as you are not around to stop them, they are likely to eat as many as they can. They may even eat more than is comfortable in case it's the last opportunity they get. When they know cookies are available on a regular basis, they are more likely to eat only as many as feels comfortable and leave the rest. This doesn't mean that you offer cookies at every meal or even every day, but it does mean you offer them regularly enough that they don't feel deprived or fearful that they'll never get enough to feel satisfied.

But what about sugar?

Sugar deserves its own section because it's a huge trigger for parents the world over. Doesn't it feel like sugar is everywhere and packaged in ways that make kids desperate for it? On top of that, we're also constantly told that sugar is bad for us and that we need to limit our intake. Chances are you've seen many of the scary articles about sugar, most of which tell only part of the story but have helped fuel the idea that we should fear it.

These mixed messages start from a young age. Has your child ever come home from school having learned that sugar is bad for them, only to be sent home days later with a flyer for a bake sale or a sugary reward for having been a good student? No wonder it's such a tricky topic for parents.

Let's unpack some myths about sugar.

Myth #1: Sugar is addictive

One of the most widely held misconceptions about sugar is that it is addictive. Registered dietician Marci Evans has been investigating the evidence and concludes that there is no scientific basis for sugar addiction. Evans argues that it's not possible to be addicted to something the human body needs for survival.

Carbohydrates are a nutrient that comes in three broad categories: sugars, starches and fibre. Sugars are simple carbohydrates and include refined sugars, like those in sweets and soft drinks, as well as natural sugars found in fruits and milk. Starches and fibre are complex carbohydrates found in foods like grains, legumes and vegetables. While the body does not specifically need highly refined sugars, it does require carbohydrates in general, as they are broken down into glucose, which is the main fuel source for the body's cells, particularly the brain and muscles. By the time glucose gets to the brain, it is impossible to tell whether it came from a lollipop or a grain of brown rice.

Evans points out that there are no potentially harmful side effects of 'coming off' refined sugar. You might feel lethargy or a slight headache, but it's not important to wean yourself off it gradually, as you have to with addictive substances. Coming off addictive drugs, including some prescription medications and even alcohol, needs to be done slowly and under medical supervision because the side effects can have catastrophic effects. That is certainly not the case for sugar.

What is true is that sugar can 'feel' addictive. It can feel like we can't stop eating it, that we can't stop thinking about it, that it has a power over us that we cannot control. So the *feeling* of addiction is very real.

The feeling of addiction, though, is not a result of the substance itself; it's a result of the *restriction* of the substance. The feeling of being out of control around sugar comes from trying to restrict or eliminate it. People who don't restrict sugar rarely feel out of control around it. For me, once I removed all limits when it came to sugar, my feelings of being addicted to it disappeared almost immediately. It was shocking to me how quickly it happened.

If your body recognises that it isn't getting enough carbohydrates (which it needs for survival), then it has mechanisms that spring into action to rectify the situation. It focuses our attention on sweet foods, finds sugary foods more desirable, or only feels satiated by something sweet.

Your body is set up to desire food just like it desires air, because food is just as necessary for survival. If you restrict what you eat and don't get enough calories or enough of what your body needs, your body will 'gasp' for food until it feels satisfied.

Please note: the system that the body uses to signal that it wants more carbohydrates is not a system dedicated solely to that purpose. The same system is employed when our bodies haven't had enough calories in general, or enough fat or protein. Indeed, it's the same system that is working quietly every day, and normally sending subtle and gentle messages. It's when we attempt to ignore or override them that the signals become dominating and loud and feel out of control.

Here's a quick exercise to demonstrate how this mechanism works. Try holding your breath for as long as you can and notice how easy it is, at first. No problem. Then it gets harder. The feeling in your chest starts to dominate your thoughts. If you're asked to do a complicated maths exercise at this point, you'll probably find you can't do it because you'll be totally preoccupied. Finally, you'll have no choice but to gasp for breath. And if you did have the willpower to ignore those increasingly intense bodily sensations – pressure in your lungs, reduced ability to think, hyperfocus on getting air – your body would end up unconscious but breathing. This doesn't mean air is addictive. It means that when you restrict it, your body starts to send signals that become louder and louder until it overrides your willpower.

Your body is set up to desire food just like it desires air, because food is just as necessary for survival. If you restrict what you eat and don't get enough calories or enough of what your body needs, your body will 'gasp' for food until it feels satisfied.

It's interesting to note that in studies testing sugar addiction in rats, addiction symptoms like bingeing, withdrawal and craving were present only when the rats had limits placed on the amount of glucose or sucrose they could access. Dr Joshua Wolrich gives a great explanation in his book *Food Isn't Medicine* of what the research into sugar addiction has found: when rats are given unlimited access to sugar, they show no signs of addictive behaviour. For rats to display addictive-like behaviour, they have to have *restricted* access to sugar.

The way the science around food and weight is presented often scares us more than it informs us.

Myth #2: Sugar is always unhealthy

When it comes to raising competent eaters, binary labels like 'healthy' and 'unhealthy' can be problematic.

If I asked you whether kiwifruit, eggs, fish or nuts were healthy, what would you say? You would probably say, yes, they're healthy. But there is a high rate of serious allergies when it comes to these foods, and for some people they are lethal. So, are they healthy?

What about carrots – healthy or unhealthy? Imagine your tween has eaten 15 carrots and made themselves unwell in the process. Is eating the next carrot a healthy or unhealthy choice? Every food on the planet has a limit at which eating it will kill you. Even water will kill you if you drink too much at one time, and yet it's fundamental to life.

Okay, then what about cupcakes? If that's all you ate for a day, you'd probably feel unwell. But what about if you've been ill and you need to restore your weight, and cupcakes are the only things you can face – are cupcakes unhealthy then?

Examples like these make it easier to see that healthy and unhealthy foods exist only in the context they are eaten. Besides, even in academic circles, there is much disagreement about what is healthy. Every other day it seems that another study comes out celebrating foods we should eat for our health or warning against those we shouldn't. It takes a high level of intellectual and scientific rigour to determine if these claims are valid.

That's why I recommend stopping the use of binary labels and treating all foods like they have a place in a healthy diet – and that includes sugar.

Myth #3: Kids can't control themselves around sugar

When I was growing up, sugar was limited in my home. But I loved sugar. I was so eager to eat it, I even chose friends based on who had homemade treats available for afternoon tea. Later, I learned to eat chocolate and lollies in secret in my bed, full of shame, under the covers where no one could see me. Unfortunately this is a common experience for people who have strict limits placed on sugar consumption.

Think about your child for a moment. Does it seem like they were born without an off-switch when it comes to sugar? Do they go crazy at parties with sweet foods on offer? If the answer to this is yes, then your child might be eating like that because they fear it will be the last time they have access to foods that taste so fabulous.

That's why I encourage you to make sugar a regular part of your child's diet, without telling your child it's bad or unhealthy. That doesn't mean you give them unbridled access to sugar 24/7. But it does mean you can allow them to enjoy it from time to time *without restriction*, as part of their wider diet. Add cookies or chocolate or sweets to a couple of morning or afternoon teatimes each week, and let them eat as much as they like during those times. Yes, you read that right. From time to time, it's important to give your child the opportunity to eat as much sweet food as is satisfying to them. It's time to put out the cookies, chocolate or sweets, and let them decide when to stop.

When you first start to do this, it might seem like your child can't stop. They might eat way more than you imagine they can. If it's too uncomfortable for you to watch, simply leave the room. Just make sure there is enough provided for them to eat until they are truly satisfied. When you return, don't comment or say anything other than letting them know you are happy they enjoyed their snack. Let them know that because they enjoyed it so much, you'll be offering it again soon and tell them when that will happen.

If your children have had severe limits put on sugar or sweet foods in your home, you might need to let them do this every day for a while, until they are completely comfortable with stopping when they've had enough and they feel confident there will always be opportunities to eat more. This is great for their eating competence, and it is entirely possible for them to learn.

How to handle dessert

I've made it pretty clear by this point that using dessert as a reward for eating veggies won't lead to the outcomes you want. This may lead you to think, *But if my kid knows dessert is coming and they only have to eat as much dinner as they like, then dessert is all they're going to want to eat.* You are not the first parent to have this concern. I certainly did.

Here's how to handle it.

1. Whenever possible, make dessert part of the meal, rather than served afterwards. In other words, put the dessert on the table, in the middle, as if it's just another dish.
2. Put only one serving on the table for each person, as you might with fish fillets or burger patties.

The exception to the rule is when dessert needs to be eaten immediately, like ice cream. If this is the case, you might say that everyone can have one scoop of ice cream as part of dinner and you can have it at any point during the meal.

It's important to make sure dessert is one regular-sized helping, so that your child can enjoy it without becoming so full that they are not motivated to try anything else.

If your child decides to eat only dessert, don't comment on it. Giving as little attention as possible to their food choices will mean they won't be eating as a way to get their attention and belonging needs met, but they will be eating to satisfy their agency, emotional and nutritional needs.

Dealing with sweet snacks when shopping with kids

Many parents brace themselves for shopping trips. It's tiresome to have your child pestering you for treats every time you go to the shop, and no one wants a tantrum at the checkout.

Here's what to do. Allocate a shopping budget for your child. Think about how much you'd normally spend in a week on sweets or ice creams while doing groceries or out and about. Then put your child in charge of that sum.

Say to your child, 'Look, I think you're old enough to choose the snacks you get when we are out of the house. I'll give you five dollars a week, and you can decide how to use it. Whether you buy a snack, a toy, or save for something bigger, it's up to you.'

Of course, five dollars in one family might be seven dollars in another; the point is you've decided the amount, but your child will decide how to spend it.

Giving your kids a spending allowance also shows that you believe they can self-regulate when it comes to buying sweets. And your trust in them will cultivate their confidence.

Since starting this book you've learned that your role is to teach your child eating competence; you're aware of your responsibilities (and your child's) when it comes to the feeding relationship; and you've got a new perspective on sugar. Now we're going to look at a wider set of parenting tools. We'll start by looking at nutrition a little differently. This is important because so many of us have an unrealistic idea of the ways nutrition is important for our health.

CHAPTER 4

New tools for your new role

Putting nutrition in perspective

When my children were born I was determined to 'do nutrition right', partly because of a misguided idea of how important nutrition is to our health. As you read this chapter, please understand that I'm not saying nutrition isn't important. It is. Eating a diet that includes fruit and vegetables has been consistently shown to have a positive impact on human health. Eating a diet made up almost entirely of refined sugar and processed foods will almost certainly have a detrimental effect. It's not that diet can't have a positive effect on human health; I want to shine a light on the extent to which it does. In fact, nutrition may not be the most important factor when it comes to your family's health.

You may have seen statistics showing that health is 80% nutrition and 20% exercise. This makes it seem like what you eat is 80% of the picture and that nothing else matters quite as much. However, this is far from reality.

According to the Centers for Disease Control and Prevention (CDC) in the United States, many factors determine health in human populations. These factors include:

- health behaviours (diet, exercise, sleep, lifestyle)
- access to medical care
- genetics
- societal characteristics and total ecology (this includes how respected and valued people feel in their community; how able people are to contribute to society in meaningful ways; the levels of marginalisation and stigma experienced in a population; the access people have to resources and help within society; and the level of socioeconomic hardship).

In their book *Body Respect*, Lindo Bacon and Lucy Aphramor show that societal characteristics and total ecology determine more than 50% of health outcomes. That leaves genetics, access to healthcare and health behaviours contributing to less than 50%. Of that amount, healthcare and genetics comprise half, while health behaviours comprise the other half. This means if a population ate some kind of

If you get anxious about what your kids are eating, it can help to remember that you are playing the long game – nutrition is very rarely an emergency.

'perfect' diet, it would still only account for less than a quarter of the long-term health outcomes of that population.

What I take from this is that it isn't helpful to have an intense focus on nutrition and exercise while neglecting the importance of social and cultural factors, and shifting our focus to other areas may indeed be beneficial.

When I first saw this information, I realised that if trying to make my children eat a certain way was neglecting their sense of autonomy and self-worth, then maybe it wasn't as strong a path to health as I had believed. This helped me chill out a bit. It helped me reorganise my priorities as a parent and gave me the confidence to show my children more trust.

Giving our children power and attention in favourable ways and helping them understand they are valued and respected for who they are on the inside can have a positive effect on their health – and make parenting a lot easier.

If you get anxious about what your kids are eating, it can help to remember that you are playing the long game – nutrition is very rarely an emergency (unless you have scurvy or are dying of starvation) and there are many, many things that can have a positive impact on your child's health over and above the food in their bellies.

Now that we have a more realistic perspective on nutrition, I want to talk more about the idea of praising versus encouraging our kids. We touched on this in the previous chapter, but I want to revisit why it's such a powerful thing to do, not just in terms of creating mealtime harmony but in all areas of your child's life.

What to do instead of praising

As we know, setting our kids up to have a strong sense of significance and belonging and to value who they are on the inside is the bedrock of raising competent eaters who believe in themselves. To build on this, I want to take a look at some common parenting practices that can actually end up working against us. Praising our kids is one of those things.

It might be hard to believe praise is counterproductive, because praise seems like it will boost confidence. We reason that if we tell our kids they are beautiful, gorgeous, awesome, amazing, smart, healthy, talented, artistic or athletic, they will believe they are or aspire to become those things. However, research suggests that praise can have the opposite effect, often discouraging them from exerting further effort or even diminishing their self-worth.

By 'praise', I mean comments that highlight achievements or hinge on external opinions. This contrasts with encouragement, which focuses on choices, behaviours or intrinsic feelings.

Imagine your child has just won a race. An example of praise would be: 'Wow – you were the fastest, that is so awesome. I'm so proud of you!' These kinds of comments link their value to results and other people's opinions of them. An example of encouragement in the same situation would be: 'You really gave it your all! You should be proud of your effort.' This emphasises their dedication and their own sense of accomplishment; that is, their opinion of themselves.

A helpful way to think about this more deeply is through the lens of internal and external value. Praise centres on external outcomes and societal judgements. Statements like, 'Your muscles look so big!' or 'Your teacher will be so proud!' tie worth to external measures.

While it's fine for your kids to know others are proud of them, it's more important that *they take pride in themselves.* This self-pride bolsters their internal value, leading to confidence and resilience.

Encouragement emphasises their personal values, virtues and feelings stemming from their actions. Phrases like, 'Your dedication is showing,' or 'Thank you for helping, even though you didn't enjoy it,' connect outcomes to their efforts, promoting internal worth.

Here are some more examples of encouragement:

- 'You've been very brave trying new things lately – it shows a lot of maturity.'
- 'The training you've put in has really paid off.'
- 'Doing that made such a difference.'

I'm not suggesting we shouldn't ever acknowledge or get excited about our child's achievements. I am suggesting we connect those achievements to actions they can repeat. Doing so will encourage their sense of internal value and motivate them to keep going.

The more kids are praised instead of encouraged, the more they will seek out external validation – recognition, status, approval, money. While these are not inherently bad things, a heavy focus on the external can lead to an unhealthy obsession with appearance and weight when their connection to their internal value is lost.

When you start to encourage instead of praise, your child might ask, 'But are you proud of me?' They may be used to relying on external validation to feel good. Please don't worry. Use phrases like, 'Of course I am, but having pride in yourself is the most important thing,' and keep focusing on encouragement.

Fascinating research backs up the idea that encouragement is a successful parenting tool. Carol Dweck, a professor of psychology at Columbia University, conducted a series of studies on 412 ten- to twelve-year-old school students in New York. The kids were taken out of class one by one and given them a set of problems to solve. Once each child finished their test, they were told their score and given feedback. One group was praised: 'That's a really good score, you must be smart at this.' The other group was encouraged: 'You must have worked really hard.'

The children were then given two options: do a more difficult problem they could learn from but might fail to complete, or do an easier task with a higher likelihood of success.

The vast majority of the students who had been encouraged – in some trials, up to 90% of them – picked the more difficult test. The kids who had been praised for looking smart mostly chose the easier test. The conclusion from the research was that when we praise kids for their intelligence, we're letting them know that the aim is to look smart, and that looking smart is preferable to challenging themselves and risking failure.

Since I started working with parents to shift from praising to encouraging their kids, I have been told of noticeable differences. A woman called Rachel emailed me after we had a conversation in a session about praise versus encouragement, and she said, 'One of the most beautiful things I've seen happen is that my ten-year-old has stopped asking if we are proud of her. When we tell her she can be proud of herself, you can see her chest puff up with pride.'

Another example came from a woman called Gaylene, whose son is a naturally talented singer. For years Gaylene had been telling him how amazing he was and how amazing his singing was. She was always so sad when he didn't want to sing in public. She would often hear him singing quietly to himself, but he was always very reluctant to sing in front of anyone else. When she encouraged his perseverance and his commitment to his singing, asking him what he liked best about it and telling him he could be super proud of himself for doing something that comes with the risk of failure, he started happily singing in front of her again. It was beautiful for Gaylene to see.

So what has this got to do with body confidence? And why are we talking about praise in a section about teaching kids to be competent eaters? Our cultural psyche when it comes to praising our kids at the dinner table runs pretty deep. *Good boy for eating your greens! You've done a fantastic job of cleaning up everything on your plate! I'm so proud of you for trying something new.*

Bear in mind that this praise might actually prevent your child from trying again. You'll do much better switching to encouragement: 'I know it's hard to try new things, but you can be proud of yourself for trying anyway.'

If this feels confusing and awkward, my suggestion is to talk about something completely unrelated to food instead. Take a moment to remind yourself that they have everything it takes to become a competent eater, and that sitting there trusting them is doing them just as much good as anything that could come out of your mouth.

Helping our children notice and respect their sense of internal value through using encouragement instead of praise can play an important role in keeping our kids safe as they transition into adulthood. When our kids are deciding whether to go on a fad diet, have sex for the first time or use drugs, they are less likely to follow the crowd, please others or try to get approval if they are used to relying on their own judgement.

Getting rid of rewards

Many of us – parents, guardians, teachers and coaches – assume that rewarding kids works in the same way we assume praise works: that it motivates kids to work hard or to change their behaviour. When I say reward, I'm referring to things like star charts, certificates and trophies, as well as handing out sweets for a job well done, paying kids for good marks at school or allowing extra screen-time for doing chores.

In the short term, rewards can indeed seem effective. They are fantastic at getting short-term obedience. However, this approach has a heavy cost. Rewarding kids can stifle genuine, long-term motivation and inadvertently signal that external recognition is more important than internal satisfaction. Take, for example, rewarding a child with an ice cream for emptying the dishwasher. The unintended message is that you don't believe the intrinsic joy of contribution to the household is sufficient for your child, they need an external reward in order to help.

Let's delve into why this happens.

Our ultimate goal is that our kids believe in their ability and are motivated by a sense of contribution and willingness to help. Rewards imply that we don't have confidence in them to do these things unless there is an external payoff.

Rewards can foster an attitude of 'what's in it for me?' When my kids were young, I noticed that rewarding them for doing chores didn't make them more likely to spontaneously pitch in. Quite the opposite happened. When I asked them to help they'd ask how much I would pay them. I didn't want to raise entitled kids, who were more interested in what was in it for them than being team players. In fact, that was the opposite of what I wanted.

Finally, and most disturbingly, rewards will suppress a child's interest in the behaviour you want to encourage. In fact, we have decades of data showing that rewards demotivate our kids more than they inspire them.

You may have heard about a study that followed preschool children who showed artistic talent. The researchers, Lepper and Greene, divided the kids into two groups. All the kids in the study were encouraged to draw, but only one group was rewarded for the drawings they produced. The kids who were rewarded showed a 50% decrease in spontaneous drawing two weeks later. Plus, the quality of the drawings the kids made declined. Something the kids used to do for the love of it turned into something they were doing for external motivation and that killed their joy.

Alfie Kohn, the author of *Punished by Rewards: The Trouble with Gold Stars, Incentive Plans, A's, Praise, and Other Bribes*, backs up this research by showing that kids who are rewarded regularly are:

- more likely to be self-centred and materialistic,
- and more influenced by external forces – peers, money, praise and recognition.

While Kohn doesn't specifically mention the pursuit of thinness, or thinness itself, as an external value, let's remember that kids who have a strong sense of internal value are less likely to be influenced by the damaging messages of diet culture: that thinness and beauty are ideals worth pursuing, regardless of their cost.

Kohn argues that ultimately only internal motivation will sustain a child's behaviour. Fortunately, we now know we can boost our child's sense of internal value by making Power Time a priority, so we can confidently ditch rewards and praise.

Why they continue behaviour you hate

By this point, you may have already begun to shift the way you approach feeding in your home. You're giving your kids the power to choose what to eat. You're encouraging instead of praising. But what happens if they continue to battle you, behave rudely and cause a fuss? You're about to learn a new way to approach bad behaviour at the table and, as a bonus, this can have a big impact elsewhere in your family life.

Bad behaviour at mealtimes can make us feel like we're failing, and we might start to wonder whether our kids will grow into horrible people. When it happens on a regular basis, it's exhausting!

Once again, I'm going to help you to shift your perspective in a helpful way.

As you've learned, Adlerian psychology tells us that our kids are motivated by two things: belonging and significance gained through attention and power. And it also tells us that our kids will get those two needs met, come what may. This means that our kids will keep using behaviour that gets their needs met – even if they hate that behaviour themselves. That's because they're getting a payoff for behaving that way.

To see how this works, think about a behaviour you'd like to change in yourself. Perhaps you've tried to implement a new habit, but it just won't stick. For instance, I wanted to start a daily morning routine so I tried all sorts of ways to get myself to walk up a steep hill every morning. I followed all the advice I could find. I'd do it every week day but then I'd make it to Saturday and I just couldn't do it anymore and I'd sleep in.

Two things were happening. I was getting loads of attention when I complained about the routine I couldn't keep, *and* I got the rest I needed because I wasn't recovering enough to handle the steep walk every single day. The payoff of resting – and the fabulous attention I received for trying to do something admirable but failing – became more important to me than the results of a consistent morning routine. In order to form a consistent morning habit, I needed to address the payoffs. I needed to get a healthy dose of attention another way – and get more rest. So I started volunteering at events I'd normally attend anyway and allowed myself to sleep in twice a week.

Let's go through an example of how this might play out for your kids. You've begun putting meals in the middle of the table, allowing your children the autonomy of serving themselves. You're training your kids on table etiquette and talking to them instead of focusing on what they are eating. Despite these positive changes, battles are still erupting between siblings. Dinners end with you losing your cool and a tense atmosphere in the house.

Often, in this instance, our instinct is to deal with the overt behaviour. But what if we changed our perspective? What if, instead of seeing bad behaviour, we see kids getting an important need met?

Could we take a moment to ponder: what payoff are they receiving? Are they getting all their attention and power needs met? Has something happened – at home or school – where they have felt a break in belonging?

We can shift our response accordingly when we understand our child is attempting to get their needs met rather than behaving badly. We can look at what the payoff is for that behaviour instead of attempting to correct it. Then we can ask them what they need. Perhaps we can give them a bonus Power Time. Or talk about what's happened during their day. Maybe they simply need compassion, a hug and a reminder they belong.

Maybe they simply need compassion, a hug and a reminder they belong.

A quiet caution

Up to this point, we have looked at tools and techniques for helping your child become a competent eater. These are great tools, but they are almost useless in the long run unless we are prepared to face the reality of a deeper, more hidden issue that affects all of us.

In the next section, I'll share the part of my learning that was the most challenging for me. I sometimes felt sick with shame and sometimes liberated beyond recognition, often within minutes of each other. These reactions came from learning that my internalised beliefs about bodies and my conclusions about what being fat meant were almost entirely based on false information.

Summary of Section One

- Our kids need appropriate attention and power in order to develop a strong sense of belonging and significance. They hook their identity more to their internal value and less to external values when they get enough appropriate power.
- Children eat for three reasons – agency, emotional and nutritional satisfaction.
- Our role is to raise competent eaters. A competent eater knows how to nourish themselves, doesn't overthink food and eats the same way whether we are observing them or not.
- Nutrition is one of many health determinants and is best seen from a wide and long-term perspective.

- Sugar can be part of a healthy diet: it doesn't have to be feared and children can learn to self-regulate their intake.
- The way we get our power will affect how enjoyable our interactions with our kids are.

Parenting tips

- Implement Power Time appropriate to your child's age.
- Be a 'good boss'.
- Give your child plenty of appropriate attention and power, and focus on boosting their internal value.
- Stick to your feeding responsibilities and give your child the responsibility to choose what and how much goes in their mouth without making comments.
- Put food in the middle of the table and allow everyone to take what they like.
- Give plenty of opportunities to eat sugar.
- Avoid using praise and rewards and use encouragement instead.

SECTION TWO

Fat

Allie is a mother of three who teaches yoga at an airy, light-filled studio, mainly during school hours. Her clients are wellness followers doing their best to be as healthy as possible. Before they get down to the business of yoga, though, Allie often begins her class with three questions. She starts by asking, 'Who loves humanity?' Usually, every hand in the room goes up. Her second question is: 'Who loves diversity in humanity?' Every hand in the room goes up again. Her third question is: 'Who loves what makes their body size or shape different from everyone else's?' This time, no hands go up. At which point Allie says, 'Then we have a problem.'

The problem? These yoga enthusiasts honestly believe that it's important to embrace diversity, as long as we're not talking about body size or shape.

If you've been testing out your newly learned eating competence tools, you may be starting to notice happier mealtimes and kids with more confidence. How good is that?

However, you may also notice that your child is eating more foods that you've been taught should be eaten only in limited ways. Watching them eat like this, you might be wondering if they'll ever eat more vegetables or become less interested in the stuff that, quite frankly, has very little nutritional value.

You may also be scared they'll put on weight, or maybe they already have. Perhaps you're having uncomfortable thoughts. *Will they be ostracised, teased or bullied? Will our GP tell me off? What will my friends think?*

If you're anything like me, these feelings made me question if I was being a bad parent. All I wanted to do was protect them from pain and I was worried that I wasn't doing enough.

These common fears can make it hard to use the tools from the previous section. One of my biggest struggles over the years has been deciding to use the tools, then freaking out and reverting to old ways. If you've noticed yourself doing this, please cut yourself a break. You are going against many deeply held cultural beliefs, and it's not surprising that you're finding it a challenge.

This section looks at why so many of us struggle, and why the concerns I mentioned above are so common. We'll uncover a hidden challenge that makes it hard to fully loosen our grip on what our child eats and to trust them to figure out what works best for them.

It goes right to the heart of what Allie teaches in her yoga class, and it's what you are going to learn yourself. Until we can be comfortable with the fact that all bodies are different – including the fact that some are fat – and recognise that it's our job to change our cultural conversations and not to control our children's bodies, it's impossible to trust a child to be at the helm of what they eat without interfering.

As you read this section, you may feel as challenged and confronted as I did when I first learned some of these concepts. I encourage you to notice and be okay with whatever comes up. Keep coming back to the question, *Is the status quo working?* Consider whether you are willing to challenge yourself and be part of changing that status quo, so that your children can grow up with a very different experience of the world than you did.

This brings us to the central theme upon which this section rests. Do you have the courage to help manifest what I believe we all hope for: a world where each and every person is respected for who they are as a person, not what they look like?

If the answer is: *Yes, that is exactly what I'd like to do*, then that requires doing something that at this point in human history is both brave and uncommonly kind: to question your ideas and beliefs about weight, and to adopt a new perspective.

CHAPTER 5

A short history of the body mass index

Jacinta is the mother of a particularly wilful 11-year-old girl named Billie. They have a family history of heart disease, and Jacinta's mother died in her late sixties from complications due to diabetes. So, not surprisingly, Jacinta wanted to do all she could to help her daughter avoid these illnesses.

In my first session with Jacinta, she told me that Billie was putting on weight. Throughout childhood, she had been an average size, but as she entered puberty, she got noticeably bigger than her peers and it made Jacinta and Billie's healthcare providers nervous. Ever since Billie was a baby, healthcare providers had warned Jacinta about the dangers of Billie putting on weight because of her family history; they advised her not to 'let' Billie get too big. The concern was that if Billie's body mass index (BMI) increased to the overweight or obese range, she would be at greater risk of heart disease and diabetes. Jacinta wanted to ensure that didn't happen, so as Billie's weight crept up, Jacinta did all she could to help Billie manage it.

Jacinta told me her concern about Billie's weight was to do with her family history rather than body image. As a slight woman whose weight had never fluctuated much, Jacinta had no personal experience of body-image struggles. However, she wasn't oblivious to the fact that these issues exist, and she did want her daughter to feel good about her body. Jacinta came to me because the new food rules she had introduced to help her daughter manage her weight weren't eliciting the results she had imagined they would. Instead of Billie eating fewer carbohydrates, fewer snacks and more veggies, she had been sneaking food and defiantly making round after round of toast, even after being told to stop. Jacinta said with exasperation, 'I'd literally have to lock the cupboards to make her follow the rules, but that just seems wrong.'

So Jacinta and I started at the same place this book begins, by discussing eating competence and the three reasons that kids eat, and then we looked at how flawed the BMI is when it comes to measuring health.

BMI = weight kg/height m^2

The BMI, or body mass index, is a simple formula to measure an individual's height-to-weight ratio. The calculation is simply weight in kilograms divided by height in metres squared. Health

The BMI has never been shown to give reliable information about someone's individual health and was not designed for that purpose.

professionals commonly use BMI as a general measurement of health. In medical terms, an individual's BMI determines whether they are classified as underweight, healthy weight, overweight or obese. These classifications are then used to predict the individual's risk of poor health outcomes.

But can the BMI really be relied upon as an accurate predictor of health outcomes? Let's be clear about this. The BMI can only tell us where an individual sits size-wise relative to the rest of the population. The BMI does not measure how much fat someone has, where it exists on their body or how much muscle mass they have; it doesn't identify heart health, resting heart rate or return-to-resting heart rate, metabolic rate, blood pressure, genetic predispositions, sleep quality, blood markers, diet quality, mental wellbeing, cholesterol or any other data about an individual.

The BMI has never been shown to give reliable information about someone's individual health and was not designed for that purpose. Nonetheless, it has become a central theme for discussions in doctors' offices, impacting on diagnoses and even access to medical care in many places around the world. How on earth did that happen?

To unravel this puzzle, we must go back 200 years and consider why the BMI was developed in the first place. It all starts with a man named Adolphe Quetelet, who busied himself with astronomy, statistics, sociology and mathematics. Quetelet, by all accounts, was fitted with a great curiosity about the world, although if you've never heard his name, it's not surprising. But you have definitely heard the name of the measuring tool that stemmed from his great curiosity: Quetelet is the grandfather of the BMI.

Quetelet was born in Belgium in 1796, in an era when many people were seeking to put their country on the intellectual map. He wanted to understand human populations better, and he set out to describe the 'perfect man'. In Quetelet's mind, the perfect man was the most average or most typical man. This old-fashioned idea of perfection is starkly different to how perfection might be thought of these days. We think of it as being something extraordinary, exceptional and probably out of reach of most people. In those days, attaining perfection meant to be the most ordinary, typical and average.

Knowing what constitutes perfection, Quetelet posited, could help us obtain it, so he squared himself to this quest using the data available to him in the early 1800s. Bear in mind that, at this point in time, white men like Quetelet unapologetically believed themselves to be superior to all other humans and, thus, the only subjects worthy of study. The data sets available back then were those of marriages, deaths, height and weight of Caucasian males who lived in France and Scotland. This is not a mere example of the data sets. This was quite literally all that was available, which meant those data sets contained not a single measurement of a woman, a child, a Polynesian, Asian or African person, or anyone else who wasn't a white European male.

Quetelet's analysis resulted in many new findings. He looked for patterns, and as he did so, he plotted the ratios of height and weight on a graph and found they fit on a beautifully shaped bell curve. He called this the Quetelet Index. He imagined the State would use his index for statistical purposes. He was clear that his index was not fit for individual diagnosis, assessment or treatment. The index, he took pains to instruct, was a population-level tool, not an individual one.

After he died, Quetelet's work, with its focus on the 'perfect man', was kept alive by the proponents of eugenics, an abhorrent school of thought that argues humans should eradicate 'undesirable' folk (people with autism, dark skin, disabilities or diverse sexual orientation, for example) through mechanisms like forced sterilisations, and encourage the reproduction of 'desirable' people (white, middle-class, straight, able-bodied and wealthy). It's an idea that makes any upholder of social-justice ideals shudder in their shoes. We are only visiting the concept here to understand that these folks kept Quetelet's Index alive and well until insurance companies stepped in.

In the late 1800s, American life insurance companies began to create their own height and weight tables, which were used to charge higher fees to policyholders who had a higher weight. Within a few years, height and weight charts became standard practice within the industry. It's important to note at this point that no research was undertaken to see if fatness was causing health issues for fatter folks; establishing this idea as fact would have required more data than was available.

It will come as no surprise that charging people with a higher weight more for their insurance policies was a winning strategy within the insurance industry. But because there was no data to specify the weight at which actual health concerns kick in, companies simply created their own tables – some charts differed by as much as 18 kilos. An individual, therefore, might have been deemed overweight according to one company's standard and a healthy weight according to another's.

The era of standardised tables begins

In 1942, the industry as a whole decided to standardise these tables. As a result, some doctors began to use the charts in their practices to measure individual health, even though the tables had no science behind them and had been created by insurance company employees, not medical researchers.

Once enough doctors had started to use the charts, calls for a unified national system began to sound. The person tasked with creating such a system was a chap called Ancel Keys, a physiologist, nutritionist and public health scientist. He was also known for his vociferous dislike of fat people. He called them disgusting, a hazard to health and – I shudder even writing this – 'ethically repugnant'. With that prejudice at the forefront, he took on the task of measuring the size and shape of the global population as a whole to figure out how to create a chart for all.

Keys got down to business by looking for the easiest ways for a doctor to measure someone's body fat while they were in their consulting room. Just think about that for a minute. He didn't start by looking for ways to effectively measure health or even the most effective way to measure body fat. He was looking for the easiest ways for doctors to measure body fat in the convenience of their offices.

He conducted a study on 7500 predominately white men from five countries (the data from the few people of colour who were measured was removed from the study – but that's a whole other story). Keys put three methods of measuring fat to the test. Two methods were rejected as ineffective; the remaining one was Quetelet's Index.

Keys himself said that the science behind Quetelet's Index wasn't perfect and didn't tell us about health. He even admitted that Quetelet's Index was chosen because it was the strongest of three weak and imperfect measures of fatness. He also said that Quetelet's Index is *only right about half of the time* when it comes to measuring obesity. It is only 50% accurate in terms of how much fat you have on your body relative to other people, which means it is entirely possible for someone in the 'obese' range to have less body fat than someone in the 'healthy weight' range.

Nonetheless, instead of accepting that measuring fatness was tricky and inaccurate and doesn't really tell us anything about anybody's individual health anyway (only about size relative to the rest of the population), Keys decided that it was the best system we had for measuring body fat.

I mean, it's convenient. Doctors find it easy to use. It's simple, and people can understand it.

In other words, Keys decided that Quetelet's Index was good enough for his goals of ease and cost-effectiveness and renamed it the body mass index (BMI).

Let's not forget that Quetelet's original data set was comprised solely of information about European men. Yet today, the BMI is a measure used indiscriminately for everyone, worldwide: a tradition that started its life with Quetelet's mission and hasn't since been rectified. Every year, South Pacific nations dominate the list of the top ten most obese countries in the world. Taking that claim at face value, it may appear that those populations are also the most unhealthy. And yet neither the measurements of South Pacific people nor the health of a South Pacific nation were ever examined when developing the BMI. Not by Quetelet's system, and not by any subsequent iterations. Sadly for all of us, this is just one of the startling problems with the BMI as an individual health measure.

The BMI we use as a diagnostic medical tool today is basically the same, with the addition of a terrible travesty that happened in 1995. But we are getting ahead of ourselves. There are some critical turns of events along the way that you need to understand.

In the years following Keys' work, research demonstrated a correlation between higher-weight bodies and poor health outcomes. There was still no evidence to suggest higher weight *caused* health outcomes, but that is a topic so important to this discussion it's going to get its own chapter.

Then in 1995, the World Health Organization decided the BMI would be the new global standard for classifying bodies according to weight. In doing so, they made some controversial assumptions – at least that's what many researchers and healthcare providers believe.

Children and the BMI

The World Health Organization also decided that the BMI was a good measure to use for children. Prior to this, it had only been used as a measure for adults because, of course, only adults – scratch that – only *white men* had been used in the studies that created the BMI.

For the World Health Organization to make this decision, it would be reasonable to expect that new evidence had come to hand: for instance, data collected from children, at the very least. That was not the case. No new data sets had been gathered, and no research was undertaken on children to see if increased size caused detrimental health outcomes. They simply took the formula used to calculate BMI in adults and applied it to kids. In other words, they did what any good scientist would guard against: they extrapolated.

As any parent knows, a child's weight can fluctuate wildly as they grow, so it's tough to tell if a child classified as overweight at age four will be overweight at six. But more importantly, in 1995, we simply didn't have data to prove childhood BMI would determine health problems later in life – and we still don't.

Fiddling with the measurements

The other extraordinary thing the World Health Organization did was to change how BMI categories were calculated. In the 1970s, a man with a BMI of 27.5 was considered overweight. In 1995, the World Health Organization changed the threshold to what it is today: 25 for adults of all genders, and at the same time they included kids as well. This change meant that millions more people were suddenly considered overweight or obese, even though their size or health had not changed.

Once again, this was not based on any science about health or weight but was done to make things easier in the doctor's office (a calculation using round numbers was simpler than one with decimal points). I am hammering this point home because it's so important. The BMI categories were never based on information that could suggest *relative health risk* to an individual, only *fatness* relative to other people.

When the World Health Organization made these decisions, many health and weight researchers suggested increasing BMI thresholds. They urged caution over the World Health Organization's decisions to decrease them, arguing that many people – particularly children – can be healthy at higher weights.

Not only did the World Health Organization lower thresholds instead of increase them, but in 1998 the US and the world followed suit. As CNN so aptly put it: 'Millions of Americans became "fat", Wednesday – even if they didn't gain a pound.' The only thing that had changed was the label afforded to their height-to-weight ratio. It was reported as if a wave of illness was spreading across the country, making the population sicker and suddenly at risk of shorter life-spans. The only thing that had changed was that the numbers had been adjusted to make it easier to measure.

The reporting opened the floodgates for millions to be spent on studying the supposed 'obesity epidemic'. Commentators and those well versed in sound research methodology (studies that give us meaningful information) have pointed out that much 'obesity epidemic' research is conducted from a starting position of 'knowing' fat is bad for us and looking to science to tell us why. Conducting research that sets out to prove a theory rather than test a theory is considered bad practice due to the poor quality of data that is collected.

But what about fatness being correlated with poor health outcomes? Regardless of the profoundly flawed history of the BMI and its dubious ability to tell anyone much about their personal health, there is research that links health issues and higher weight (at a population level). However, we also know of other factors that correlate much more closely with health outcomes than fatness. Here are a few:

- Doing 30 minutes of exercise a few times a week.
- Eating a varied diet rich in fruit and vegetables.
- Receiving respectful healthcare. (Many higher-weight people report putting off medical appointments because they don't feel as though they are taken seriously. Regardless of their symptoms, they might be reminded that they are fat, scolded for not losing weight and prescribed weight loss.)
- Improving socio-economic conditions. (You may have heard the well-known aphorism that in the greater London area, for every tube stop between the centre of London and your home, your health outcomes decrease.)

While there may be economic or social barriers to achieving the points above, they are each possible regardless of someone's BMI and can improve health outcomes even if the BMI doesn't change.

Some commentators argue that it's easier for governments to tick a box to say that the medical system has this obesity problem under control than to tackle the arduous task of creating policy changes that could make a real difference. It's demonstrably harder to ensure everyone has access to fresh vegetables at affordable prices, a way to store them, the know-how to cook them, access to safe green spaces to exercise in, enough time to prepare food, enough sleep and good-quality healthcare – even though we have evidence that all of the above can make a measurable difference at a population level. Regardless of the BMI profile of that population, those things are truly hard and expensive to implement.

When I learned the real story of the BMI, I wanted to throw things. I had been steadfast in my dedication to keeping myself and my children at a 'healthy weight' and the index I'd judged us against was built on – what? Certainly not rigorous science. I felt sick to my stomach, and I had the privilege of having a BMI in the 'healthy' range. What must it be like to be someone who lives at a higher weight? I don't have that lived experience, but the more I listened to those who did, the more I had an understanding of the cost and toll it took on their lives.

So what did I do with that anger and frustration? More digging. What else had I believed to be true that was not so clear-cut? As it turns out, a lot! And what could I do to stop myself from making these kinds of false assumptions in other areas?

The answer took me right back to my university days when my lecturer stood at the head of my research methods class and said, 'A good scientific researcher will never confuse causation with correlation.' Returning to those two C words gave me something to work with, and I want to share what I learned with you.

CHAPTER 6

Correlation vs causation

When I relayed the history of the BMI to Billie's mum, Jacinta, she also felt dismayed and frustrated at the lack of scientific integrity around what the BMI was telling her. But that wasn't enough to stop her from worrying about her child's weight.

'We are talking about a child with a very clear family history here, Emma, and if she grows into a fat adult, I've been told she will be at terrible risk,' Jacinta said to me. 'I can see what you are saying about eating competence and the sketchy ability of the BMI to tell us anything meaningful, but it's not enough. I need a lot more surety that taking my focus off her weight won't be a bad move.'

I agreed. It wasn't enough. Not even close. But having a new appreciation of the relationship between fatness and health would take Jacinta a huge step closer to making informed decisions for her child.

Before we go down that road, I want to give you a little more context about Billie's health. Aside from her recently increasing BMI, every other screening test showed that Billie's health was fine. Her blood pressure, cholesterol and blood lipids were within the expected range, and she had no signs of diabetes. She swam twice a week and played touch rugby on the weekends. She enjoyed eating foods from all food groups and slept well at night. The BMI – a measure that was never based on information gathered from children or women, and that researchers have admitted is wrong about relative fatness 50% of the time – was the only measure being used to suggest that Billie's health was at risk.

With that picture of Billie's current health in mind, what Jacinta really wanted to know was whether fatness would cause health problems for Billie *in the future*. If she could help Billie lose weight in her youth, would that protect her from diabetes and heart disease later?

Looking at it another way, Jacinta needed to know whether Billie's weight gain might cause her to get heart disease and/or diabetes, or whether something else might cause the kinds of health issues that are separate and distinct from weight but often present in those who are bigger.

Remember those two C words my enthusiastic research methodology lecturer told me about all those years ago? Understanding the difference between *correlation* and *causation* in the context of health and wellbeing studies is vital for any parent who wants to make informed decisions about their child's health.

What is correlation, and how is it different from causation?

Correlation is a connection. When one thing happens, so does something else, but one doesn't necessarily lead to the other happening – there is a third, sometimes hidden, factor at play.

Yellow teeth, for instance, are correlated with lung cancer. As you know, yellow teeth don't cause lung cancer – cigarette smoking causes both yellow teeth and cancer. Ice-cream consumption and drowning are correlated, but eating ice cream obviously doesn't cause drowning. Summer causes both swimming and ice-cream consumption, but drowning is caused by one of many factors unrelated to ice cream.

That third factor isn't always easy to see, especially in the case of weight and health.

Underweight BMI is correlated with early death and is just as correlated to poor health outcomes as the obese BMI category. When I share this fact with people, it is easy for them to see why a low BMI *correlates* with poor health outcomes but is not the *cause*. After all, weight loss – and ultimately an underweight BMI – is a symptom of many terminal illnesses, so it's pretty easy to see that in those instances the cause of death is the underlying health condition, not the low BMI.

My own dear mother, for example, became emaciated with the onset of motor neurone disease. Her weight loss didn't cause her eventual death, but significant and quick weight loss like she experienced undoubtedly occurred at the same time as the underlying reasons for her death. Imagine if her healthcare providers had waited for her to follow a weight-restoration diet before they were willing to do more tests. Imagine if she stood up for herself and said, 'It's not the weight, something else is going on,' and was then thought of as a difficult and non-compliant patient, and had her treatment options compromised. My mother didn't experience any of that. But many bigger-bodied parents who attend my speaking events tell me they have been called 'non-compliant' and told that they must lose weight before any diagnostic tests can be ordered.

Jacinta got pretty upset thinking that her child might encounter an interaction like this with a healthcare provider.

The conversation becomes a lot trickier when the script is flipped. When I ask people to consider that a higher BMI could well be correlated with health issues in the same way that a low BMI is (that is, not the cause of health issues in and of itself but simply occuring at the same time), all sorts of 'yeah buts' and 'what ifs' and 'what abouts' pop up. It becomes much, much harder for people to accept that fat itself might not be the problem.

Let me lighten the mood here for a moment and share some truly hilarious correlations. I want to make it very clear how useless it is to focus on eliminating correlated health conditions as a way to fix a problem.

Having a master's degree means you'll die ten years younger than if you have a PhD (so should we warn folks against undertaking a single graduate degree, for their health?). Margarine consumption in Maine, USA, correlates with that state's divorce rates. People who have the most sex earn the most money.

While those examples are as harmless as they are funny (because no one is suggesting we ban margarine in Maine to save relationships from breaking down), it is harmful when we try to use a correlated health condition to fix an underlying cause. Whitening yellow teeth is not a great approach to healing lung cancer, and banning ice cream is not going to help decrease drowning rates.

Here's another example. Healthcare providers know that male pattern baldness is correlated strongly with prostate cancer. Ragen Chastain, who writes an impeccably researched newsletter about weight and healthcare, asks us to imagine what would happen if the health system became completely focused on the prevention of balding and the personal responsibility of people with prostates to grow their hair back, instead of screening and testing for prostate cancer. Eventually we'd see 'War on Baldness' headlines in newspapers and a glut of useless but profitable hair-growth remedies being offered for sale. We'd see the purveyors of those remedies sitting on healthcare boards created with the express purpose of eradicating balding. A cultural belief would emerge. If we could just get all those lazy bald folk to take some pride in themselves and grow their hair back, imagine the health costs we'd save!

This, Ragen argues, is what is happening with health issues faced by bigger people. While we are busy trying to eliminate a human characteristic – fatness – that is correlated with certain health conditions, many people are receiving poor treatment and getting much sicker than they would if we stopped trying to fix their fatness. Not to mention the fact that people blame them for failing

When studies are reported as if correlations are a 'cause' (*Margarine Causes Divorce!*), the public can get the wrong end of the stick, and it is notoriously difficult to reverse public opinion once it has been formed.

to make themselves slim, rather than blaming the interventions that don't work.

Causation, on the other hand, is just what it sounds like. It is the thing that has a direct impact on the outcome. The important thing to remember is that it can be a difficult job to tease out the difference between correlations and causes. And it can be disastrous to get them mixed up.

Much of the problem rests in scientific reporting rather than the studies themselves. When studies are reported as if correlations are a 'cause' (*Margarine Causes Divorce!*), the public can get the wrong end of the stick, and it is notoriously difficult to reverse public opinion once it has been formed.

Jacinta decided she really needed to understand whether the research identifying fatness as the root cause of heart disease and diabetes was rigorously ruling out correlations. Without that information, she wouldn't know if she was fighting hard to ban ice cream in a fruitless attempt to stop her daughter from drowning. And in giving all her energy and effort to the ice cream, she might be failing to focus on something far more important: providing swimming lessons. She wasn't about to let that happen.

How to tell good science from bad

I asked Jacinta if she'd like to gain a few more skills in the pursuit of separating good science from bad in the realm of food and weight studies. I told her that it was okay to say no to this. Some folks do say no; they'd prefer to trust others to do that for them. She said yes. And I'm going to assume you do too.

- *Peer review* – This is a process whereby experts in a field critically evaluate a study before it is published to check that it is rigorous and credible, and that it contributes valuable knowledge. The reviewers scrutinise the study's design, methodology, data analysis and conclusions. Peer review helps maintain high scientific standards and prevents the dissemination of inaccurate or misleading findings. Ideally, peer reviews will be conducted by individuals outside of the organisation that funded the research.
- *Double-blind studies* – In these studies, participants don't know which intervention they are receiving, so that they don't have a preconceived idea of what the outcome should be. Conducting double-blind food and nutrition research poses unique challenges, primarily because it's difficult to mask the intervention. Unlike a pill, which can be made to look and taste the same whether it's a placebo or drug, foods have distinctive tastes, textures and smells, making it nearly impossible to find perfect stand-ins. Dietary interventions often involve lifestyle changes that participants are fully aware of, such as eating more fruits and vegetables or limiting processed foods, which inherently negates the 'blindness' of the

study. The impact of food and nutrition on health often requires long-term studies to show meaningful results, but the longer the study, the higher the chance of non-compliance or changes in other lifestyle factors, which complicates the study.

- *Rat studies* – Studies on rats are useful for initial studies that tell us if more research needs to be done on humans. However, using rat studies to claim what will happen in humans is irresponsible.
- *Self-reported data* – There are several limitations to participants' self-reported data when it comes to weight and nutrition studies. Respondents can unintentionally misreport what they eat because they've forgotten or have misunderstood the portion sizes. There can also be intentional misreporting due to social desirability bias, where participants alter their responses so they will be viewed favourably. This can lead to both underestimations and overestimations of calorie intake, weight and exercise levels. Additionally, self-reporting often fails to account for day-to-day variations in diet and activity levels, which can significantly impact a study's accuracy.
- *Reverting to mean* – A portion of the population will experience symptom improvement without any intervention – that is, the problem resolves itself on its own. This is known as returning to mean. Because there

is always a percentage of the population that will return to mean, we need to study many people to prove that an intervention works.

- *The placebo effect* – This is when a healing event happens following an intervention that couldn't have caused the healing; for example, when a heart starts beating in rhythm following the insertion of a pacemaker but the pacemaker doesn't have a working battery. It's important to understand the percentage of people who will experience the placebo effect in any study.
- *Control group* – A group of participants in a study who don't receive the actual intervention; for example, they get sugar pills instead of the medicine being tested. The control group tells us how many people heal via the placebo effect.
- *N number* – The number of participants in a study. A study with fewer than 600 participants does not provide statistically meaningful results. Much health and wellness evidence is based on an *n* of one, meaning just one person said, 'I did such and such and got such and such result.' This can sound compelling, but it does nothing to say what result *you* will have if you do the same thing.
- *Anecdotes vs data* – When someone does something and experiences a change, that is an anecdote and tells us nothing about the efficacy of the intervention. If I take

vitamin C and my cold clears up, it's tempting to think the vitamin C 'worked'. In reality, it may or may not have worked; there is no way to tell. Anecdotes might indicate that more study is needed, but they don't tell us anything more than that. Data, on the other hand, is collected from multiple instances, under controlled conditions and uses large sample sizes to discern patterns and trends. Unlike a single personal experience, data provides statistical evidence that can be analysed to draw valid conclusions.

- *Testing vs proving a theory* – Research that sets out to *prove* a theory, rather than *test* a theory, is flawed from the get-go. Setting up studies to prove that carrots are good for me will lead me to avoid any research that might show carrots have a detrimental effect on me. Testing the effect of carrots on my health will provide more meaningful results.
- *Repeatable* – Unless a study is repeatable, it doesn't provide meaningful results. That is why scientific studies are repeated: to make sure the same results are generated, or to determine whether a new study method needs to be developed.

The limits of nutrition and weight research

Weight-loss studies are notorious for excluding the data gathered from any participants who drop out of the study while it is in progress. It's common to find weight-loss studies reporting 'success' with a certain method, but when you include participants who have dropped out, the success rate is vastly reduced. It's safe to say that those who successfully lose weight during weight-loss studies do not drop out.

Weight-loss studies must be conducted over at least five years in order to gain an understanding of long-term success. Weight loss is easy to achieve with almost any intervention in the first six weeks because short-term weight loss is relatively easy to achieve. Once the body has detected weight loss, though, it switches on its weight-regain systems. It's what happens after five or ten years that shows long-term efficacy.

Understanding who is paying for research is important. Good science based on sound methodology that gets the same results regardless of who conducts it isn't affected by who is funding it. However – and this is a 'however' of the grandest proportions – bad science is often conducted when the biases of a financial backer get in the way. If the financial backer wants to 'prove' rather than 'test' a theory, because proof of said theory would be lucrative, that is a major red flag. That is why external peer review is crucial to the validity of scientific studies. The other reason it's good to understand where funding comes from is so that we can pick up on bias in the reporting of results.

Be mindful of real numbers versus percentages versus statistically meaningful numbers. Learning that a particular food increases the risk of colon cancer by 300% sounds terrifying, but learning that a particular food increases your risk of colon cancer from 1 in 10 million to 3 in 10 million isn't such a worry. A weight-loss drug may be able to show statistically significant weight loss after two years, but that weight loss might not be such that anyone would notice. If a weight-loss drug is shown to be the cause of a 5-kilogram weight reduction in someone who is 250 kilograms, that weight loss will be deemed statistically significant. Whether a 5-kilogram reduction is noticeable or could have a meaningful effect on someone's health remains to be proven. In statistics, 'significant' doesn't mean 'noticeable' or 'meaningful', it just means that it's almost certainly caused by the intervention.

* * *

With this knowledge, a whole new world opened up to Jacinta. She wanted to examine whether fat really did cause health issues. If so, how do we know that? Is the information based on good science?

And the two biggest questions she wanted to answer were these: *If fatness is not the cause of a health issue, then what is causing it? And, more importantly, are those causes being addressed?*

These are the questions we'll look at next.

CHAPTER 7

A new perspective on health and weight

If we are going to trust our kids to eat what is right for them without overthinking and to make the same choices whether someone is observing them or not, then we need to have a better handle on the relationship between weight and health.

Now that you understand the important distinction between correlation and causation and you've learned some ways to check if studies are undertaken using good methodology, it's time to consider whether fat tissue itself is the cause of ill health, or if it has a different kind of relationship with health. If we want our kids to experience joy and harmony with their bodies, and we don't want to keep freaking out and sticking our oars in, this section of the book is a must-read.

To begin, I want to look at three commonly held assumptions that, under inspection, aren't as accurate as we've been led to believe.

Assumption #1: Long-term weight loss is achievable; you just need the right diet (or lifestyle change) and the right motivation

You've no doubt heard the phrase 'diets don't work'. The thing about this, though, is that it is taken to mean that if you want to lose weight, you shouldn't go on a diet – what you really need is a lifestyle or mindset change.

What 'diets don't work' means in reality is that long-term weight loss isn't possible for the vast majority of people. That's a very different idea, and one of great importance.

Take a moment to think about people you know who have gone on a diet. How many have lost a noticeable amount of weight and kept it off from that one diet? Now think about the people who lost weight but eventually put it back on, and perhaps ended up bigger than they started. How many had no change in weight? And how many kept the weight off, but to do so they had to continue to restrict what they eat?

By age 45, the average British woman has embarked on 61 diets. If weight loss worked in the long run, why the need for so many diets? Research also tells us that if you are in the 'obese' BMI category, the chance of achieving a 'healthy' weight, even for a short period of time, is 1 in 210 if you are a man and 1 in 124 if you are a woman. That's less than a 1% chance. And that is not because folks with an obese BMI do not attempt weight loss.

The other thing research tells us is that after three to five years, 95–98% of dieters will regain all the weight they lost. The frustrating thing about this is that the people who are most likely to succeed on a diet (the 2–5%) tend to be the ones who are naturally thin in the first place. Perhaps they've put on a little weight due to unusual circumstances, so they go on a diet and return to their typical size. In my experience, they seem to be the ones who find it the most challenging to acknowledge that weight loss doesn't work for bigger people.

Now, let's look at the assumption that motivation is a major factor in losing weight. If you google 'how do I lose weight' (and I suggest you don't, or at least do it incognito or you'll be flooded with advertisements from weight-loss companies) or spend a few minutes on social media looking at accounts of wellness influencers, you'll find innumerable offers of help with the mindset, goals and accountability required for the pursuit of weight loss. The messages these businesses trumpet are as persistent as they are consistent. *Weight loss works but, if it hasn't so far, the problem isn't weight loss itself: it's that you have a mindset problem. But don't worry, it's not your fault. If you follow our suggestions, the weight will fall off.*

Spoiler alert: there is nothing wrong with our collective motivation. People who attempt to lose weight and fail are generally not lazy, uninterested in their health or lacking in stickability. The problem isn't in the mind. The problem is this: weight loss doesn't work for everyone, just like some physio adjustments don't work for everyone. If an individual doesn't respond to a particular type of physical therapy, we don't assume they have a mindset problem; the problem is that the therapy doesn't work for them.

So if we don't have a collective mindset problem, then achieving weight loss must be about finding the right lifestyle change or dietary habits, right? No, as it happens, the problem and the message are the same. *Don't worry if you haven't been able to lose weight and keep it off before, you just didn't know about this diet, this food or this way of exercising! Follow me and the kilos will fall off, forever.* But those claims, even if they're accompanied by real anecdotes, cannot be backed up by sound research.

No matter how many different lifestyle, dietary and mindset changes humans have tried over the years – and humans have been at it for the best part of 100 years – the fact remains that only 2–5% of people achieve lasting long-term weight loss, and collectively, we get fatter every year.

But so what? What's the harm if our kids want to lose some weight, even if only temporarily? Isn't losing weight good for us, so even if they put it back on, surely that can't be a problem? Well, let's see.

Assumption #2: Weight loss comes with no downside

When weight loss is discussed, it's almost always in glowing, reverential terms. There is an unquestioned belief that weight loss is fundamentally good for us. If someone loses weight, how often do other folks express concern about that person's health? How many clear warning signs accompany weight-loss regimes, encouraging folks to proceed with caution? None and none.

Instead, the overarching, immediate conclusion is that weight loss is a golden ticket. It guarantees improved wellbeing, confidence, longevity, self-esteem – things we'd all be happy for our children to experience.

So really, downsides? What downsides?

To answer that question we are going to begin by looking at the work of Dr Cynthia Bulik, the founding director of the University of North Carolina's Center of Excellence for Eating Disorders. In a presentation Bulik gave at Otago University in 2015, she outlined how dieting can trigger an eating disorder. Here's what happens when 100 11-year-olds are put on a diet. The diet itself doesn't matter. It could be anything from traditional calorie-counting to more modern lifestyle- and mindset-change approaches. Regardless of the 'how', the same picture emerges when – and this is the important part – the intention of the dietary changes is weight loss.

Out of the 100 children who were put on a diet:

- **One will develop anorexia**. Until recently, anorexia had the highest mortality rate of all psychiatric illnesses (it was overtaken by opioid addiction in 2019). Some of the saddest stories I hear are from parents describing their shock at the dire prognosis for their child when diagnosed with anorexia. Parents are bewildered, confused and terrified. They routinely tell me they get almost no support from friends and family. There is a kind of 'oh, they'll come right' attitude. There isn't the sense of support that one would expect when their child has been diagnosed with a potentially fatal illness.
- **Three to four will develop a binge-eating disorder**. This includes bulimia and other binge-eating disorders. The

mortality rate is not as high as with anorexia, but it's up there.

- **Ninety of those kids will go on to have a lifelong struggle with yo-yo dieting.** Yo-yo dieting is losing weight and putting it back on, and sometimes gaining more weight in the process. Yo-yo dieting is often accompanied by body shame and self-loathing. This makes sense when you think about the average 45-year-old woman who has tried 61 diets. Many parents tell me about the struggle they have had of losing weight only to gain it back and how this makes them feel like a failure. It's this experience that often drives parents to want their children to be effortlessly slim. If only they can help their children to eat and move in a way that prevents the need for endless dieting and hating what they see in the mirror.
- **Five will lose weight in the long term without serious long-term effects** (although some argue this weight is only kept off via disordered eating practices). If you are someone (or know someone) who has gone on a diet and lost weight easily and the weight has remained off, please remember you are the exception not the rule. Chances are, it was your first diet. Weight loss gets harder and harder to achieve the more often you attempt it. Quite possibly, you have been slim most of your life and had put on weight that was unusual for you and the diet brought

> you back to your typical size. First-timers and naturally thin folks are far more likely to succeed in weight loss than repeat dieters and those with more fat.

So, yes, five out of ten kids had long-term 'success', but 5% is a terrible efficacy rate for any health protocol. It's not a case of: *Oh, this works, but we've discovered that if people get support their odds of success are much greater.* It's not a case of: *It works for 5% of people, so keep trying until you're in the 5%.* Neither statistics nor health work that way. It's a case of: *We don't know how to help most people lose weight in the long run without potentially serious (and in some cases fatal) side effects.*

This also means that even if being thinner would be helpful to your child's health, we don't have an effective or safe way to achieve that outcome that doesn't come with the very real risk of serious, life-threatening mental illness and psychological distress.

As sad as it is true, a long-term dieter is more likely to end up with an eating disorder than sustained weight loss. Understanding this was a sobering moment for Jacinta. Ushering her daughter Billie into a lifetime of trying to control her weight was more likely to lead to Billie having an eating disorder than a lower weight. The implications of that felt very real.

Let's look at what 5% means in real numbers. If one million people go on a diet (a quick Google search says that 45 million Americans go on a diet each year), that means 50,000 people will lose weight and keep it off with minimal side effects. At face value, 50,000 looks like a huge number of 'success' stories, doesn't it? It's not until we understand that for every 50,000 successes, there are 950,000 failures that things become a little clearer. (And now times that by 45.) That is why we have to be extremely careful about believing that weight-loss anecdotes, even a seemingly large number of them, tell a typical story.

It is estimated that 9% of Americans will develop an eating disorder in their lifetime. We are not talking about some small, insignificant, minority health problem here. We are talking about 3.6 million people in the United States alone. In New Zealand it is conservatively estimated that 4% of our population live with an eating disorder (this was pre-Covid), but that number could be as high as 9%. That means somewhere between 200,000 and 450,000 people in New Zealand will have an eating disorder in their lifetime. If you or your child are one of them, you are not alone. Not by any stretch.

So why is weight loss so dangerous? Why can attempting to lose weight result in an eating disorder?

The answer is more complex and more nuanced than I can do full justice to here. However, there are two reasons to be aware of that both relate to genes and are worth touching on, even if it's just the tip of the iceberg.

Research spearheaded by Cynthia Bulik shows that genetics account for somewhere between 40% and 60% of one's likelihood of developing an eating disorder. The type of gene that Bulik's work has identified is the type of gene that needs an environmental trigger to activate it. For years, eating-disorder clinicians have highlighted the connection between clients going on diets and subsequently developing an eating disorder. While the research is still young, one risk factor being studied is whether weight loss is the primary trigger for activating those genes. If this turns out to be true, it means that intentional weight loss is *causing* eating disorders.

The second reason also relates to our genes, but a different type of gene. These genes are the reason it's so hard to lose weight and why so few people can achieve sustained long-term weight loss. It's important to understand why our bodies fight against sustained weight loss because it is directly related to weight cycling – the process of losing and gaining weight over and over. Weight cycling, as Ragen Chastain points out, is just as correlated as fatness is to all the increased health issues bigger people face. In other words, if you control for weight cycling in studies that look at health issues, thin people have the *same risk* of developing lifestyle-related disease as fatter people. Weight loss that is part of a wider picture of repeated gaining and losing has been linked to many poor health outcomes.

So let's understand the second genetic reason. These genes are the ones that create the blueprint for our bodies. These genes don't require an environmental trigger. They are the plan of how our physical bodies are designed to be expressed in the world. These genes are responsible for our individual eye colour, head shape, arm length and indeed how big or fat we get. If you imagine a graph on which you plot human size and shape of body parts within a population, you'll always come out with a bell curve. This happens with fatness in the same way it happens with height. Some of us will have very little fat and be very slight, others will have large amounts of fat and be very large.

The expression of those genes is taken very seriously by our body. It will defend our blueprint with all sorts of incredible and fascinating mechanisms. When we attempt to shrink our predestined size or shape by eating fewer calories, our body will shut down our metabolism, increase our appetite, make food taste better and hold onto fat in order to make sure we can maintain our size, in case we end up in a situation of limited available calories again in the future.

Our genes don't care if we want to look like Kate Moss, or if we have a wedding to attend, or even if our healthcare providers are getting hot under the collar about us not following their weight-loss advice. Our genes care about expressing their blueprint. That's why so many people have the experience of losing weight only to find it comes back.

Intentional weight loss can also generate a restrictive mindset, which in turn leads to an unhealthy relationship with food. When we eliminate certain foods or food groups, a binary sense of 'good' and 'bad' foods can form in our minds. This not only fosters guilt around eating, but it can also lead to an obsession with food and trigger disordered eating patterns.

Another downside of attempting weight loss is the potential for nutrient deficiencies. Restrictive diets may not provide the variety necessary for optimal nutrition. This can lead to deficiencies in essential vitamins and minerals, with consequences ranging from fatigue and weakened immunity to serious long-term health problems such as osteoporosis or anaemia.

Attempting weight loss can also promote a quick-fix mentality, often prioritising weight loss over engaging in sustainable health behaviours. While weight loss might provide temporary satisfaction, it ignores the complexity of maintaining regular health-promoting activities like physical activity, getting enough sleep, stress management and more.

Furthermore, weight loss can negatively impact mental health over and above the onset of an eating disorder. The stress of constantly monitoring food intake and body weight can lead to increased anxiety and diminished self-esteem. Feeling deprived or failing to meet weight-loss goals can contribute to feelings of failure and shame, negatively impacting overall mental wellbeing.

Physical side-effects of intentional weight loss can also be harmful. Some people may experience fatigue, dizziness, constipation or other digestive problems. These issues not only cause discomfort but can also discourage regular physical activity, further undermining long-term health.

Once I understood the vast array of downsides that can accompany intentional weight loss, I had a very different worldview – one that has helped me understand that even if losing weight had a potential positive benefit for my child, the potential costs were far too great to consider it a good idea.

Assumption #3: Fat people are always unhealthy

This assumption, it has to be said, is even more ingrained and even harder to get our heads around than the first two. We can look around us and intuitively understand that weight loss doesn't really work for most folks. I've yet to meet someone who doesn't know at least one person who has been on diets almost their entire life and only seems to get bigger. We can also see that most people stay kind of the same-ish size for most of their lives, perhaps putting a bit on as they get older. Most of us have seen the out-of-control eating disorder statistics and likely know someone who has (or has had) an eating disorder. Even though we can see all that, overturning this next assumption is far more challenging to our collective beliefs.

Remember how I wanted to throw things when I learned about the very poor science and equally dodgy history behind the BMI? Well, this assumption made me twice as upset. If you'd been a fly on my wall, you'd have heard many exclamations of, 'Seriously? You've got to be kidding!' So please pay extra attention here and feel free to shout obscenities in the shower (or something equally cathartic). You're in good company.

What you're about to learn is that fat isn't quite the problem we've been led to believe it is. In the last chapter, I promised we would unpick whether being fat really is bad for us (*causation*) or if fat is more often a third factor in a complex picture (*correlation*). Let's get into it.

We'll start with research meticulously conducted by Lindo Bacon, PhD, a researcher and author in the field of nutrition, and Lucy Aphramor, PhD, a registered dietician and critical public health scholar. In the early 2000s, they noticed the term 'obesity epidemic' being used liberally in the media. They noticed that obesity was automatically assumed to be a health problem, not just a growing phenomenon. They also noticed that a great amount of media attention focused on the dangers of obesity, but when they tried to find data to substantiate the claims, they couldn't. There were no numbers to show that an increase in body size was causing an increase in ill health. It was true that populations around the world had become bigger (the bell curve for size had shifted to the right, but it's interesting to note that every measure of human size increased at the same time, so that we became taller as well as fatter), but they couldn't find anything to show that the increase in fatness caused increases in health issues. In other words, they couldn't find evidence to substantiate claims of a health crisis.

So the researchers undertook that research themselves. They performed a metadata study that included data on two million teenagers, to look at the prevalence of diseases in the western world. They wanted to see if the prevalence of any diseases had shifted in line with an increase in fatness, and what they found was unexpected.

They boiled their findings down to the prevalence of diseases and conditions for every 100,000 teenagers. The following numbers include both preventable diseases, and conditions that cannot be prevented.

For every 100,000 teenagers:

- 340 had autism,
- 240 had cerebral palsy,
- 120 had Down syndrome,
- 15 had cancer,

- 12 had type 2 diabetes,
- and, shockingly, 2900 had an eating disorder.

Are you as surprised by those numbers as I was?

It's important to understand the difference between type 1 and type 2 diabetes because they have different causes and management strategies. Type 1 diabetes is an autoimmune condition where the body's immune system attacks and destroys the insulin-producing cells in the pancreas, leading to a lack of insulin. It often develops in childhood and requires lifelong insulin therapy. Type 2 diabetes, on the other hand, is primarily associated with insulin resistance, where the body's cells do not respond effectively to insulin. While type 2 diabetes can sometimes be managed with lifestyle changes and oral medications, it may also require insulin therapy as the disease progresses.

While we are not talking specifically about increases in those diseases and conditions, it may be interesting to note that in 20 years the instance of type 2 diabetes in teenagers has only increased by one per 100,000. One. While type 2 diabetes is preventable and the number of cases should be zero, it's hard to fathom how the term 'epidemic' (which indicates a growing health issue) took hold.

Fat is not the problem

The other thing that fired red-hot anger through my veins was realising what happens when fatness is treated like a problem to eradicate in and of itself, rather than a condition correlated with other symptoms. Not only is the 'cure' for fatness creating great harm to many folks in the form of eating disorders and psychological stress, but when a patient is diagnosed as fat and prescribed weight loss, their underlying conditions can be, and often are, missed. We go into this more in Chapter 8.

Many fat people are healthy. Many super-fat people are too. Many fat people enjoy regular exercise, eat nutritious foods, drink limited alcohol and don't smoke, get good sleep and take pride in caring for themselves. So do many thin people.

It's also true that many fat people don't eat nutritious food or exercise regularly or take much care of their health. And neither do many thin people. There is not a single disease found in fat people that isn't also found in thin people. But if a thin person gets heart disease or type 2 diabetes, they are often treated like it's terribly bad luck and are given health-behaviour suggestions that don't include weight loss. There is no research to suggest that the same behaviours, undertaken without using weight as a measure, don't make a difference in fat people.

At this point you might be thinking, *Okay, but don't fatter people experience health problems much more than thin people? Why is that?* One answer is to do with weight cycling, a concept we touched on in the section about weight loss having downsides. It's worth revisiting again here, because it also reinforces the notion that it's not necessarily fatness that is the cause of health issues in bigger people. As Bacon and Aphramor put it in their book: 'Weight cycling can account for all of the excess mortality associated with obesity in both

Many fat people are healthy. Many super-fat people are too. Many fat people enjoy regular exercise, eat nutritious foods, drink limited alcohol and don't smoke, get good sleep and take pride in caring for themselves. So do many thin people.

the Framingham Heart Study and the National Health and Nutrition Examination Survey (NHANES). It may be, therefore, that the association between weight and health risk can be better attributed to weight cycling than adiposity [fatness] itself.'

What they are essentially saying is that it's the up and down of dieting that contributes to health issues found in fatter people, not the weight itself. It makes sense, doesn't it? The people who are most likely to go on repeated diets are bigger people, which means they are most likely to be at risk for health issues associated with dieting.

A couple of years ago I saw a New Zealand documentary about a weight-loss study in which fat teenagers ate the poop of thin teenagers (pretty grim, I know). The poop was put into capsules that the fat kids swallowed each day. The idea was that the gut bacteria of the thin kids was the cause of their thinness and if the same gut environment could be transferred to the fat kids, they would lose weight. At the same time as swallowing poop pills, the teens also increased their exercise and improved the nutritional content of their diets. They also limited the calories they ate.

At the end of the documentary, the results of the study were revealed and, drum roll, the fat kids didn't lose a significant amount of weight. They did, however, improve on all sorts of other health measures. They were fitter, stronger. Their blood pressure and resting heart rates were lowered. They said they were happier. Nonetheless, the study was seen as a categorical bust.

Let's think about that for a minute. The kids' health had, indeed, improved. If fatness is the cause of ill health, how can health improve while fat remains? The point here is that health behaviours can improve health regardless of weight (and whether it goes up or down), and that focusing on weight makes us blind to what should be the most important goal: improved health.

This was a lightbulb moment for Jacinta. 'Imagine if I stopped focusing on weight as the important measure for Billie's health and started measuring other things,' she told me. 'Instead of being worried about her size, imagine if I celebrated the way she looked after her health. Imagine if instead of trying to help her eat fewer calories, I encouraged her to keep up sport, enjoy nutritious food and just forget about weight? That feels so much kinder and more empowering and ultimately healthier than trying to make sure her body is a particular size.'

I couldn't have agreed more.

One of the problems that keeps our cultural obsession with weight loss alive and kicking is the incorrect assumption that bigger people always eat more than thinner ones. And that not only do they eat more, they eat the wrong food. The belief is that if a big person eats less and eats better, weight loss will automatically follow. This is not true.

Ellyn Satter's research has shown that, contrary to common belief, fatter kids in general eat fewer calories than thinner ones. It's also been shown that if a human being improves their diet and exercise, one of three things is guaranteed to happen: they may lose weight; they may gain weight; they may not change size. There is no way to know which will happen. A person's weight is likely to stabilise after maintaining those changes for some time, but where it will stabilise is anyone's guess. I'm going to restate a point here because it's important to remember that what we eat isn't the sole determinant of our size; there are super-fat people who eat a nutritious diet, exercise regularly, feel satisfied, don't overthink food and feel good about their bodies. There are thin people with poor diets who get no exercise and don't change size. Many experts in weight science suggest this is because there are over a hundred factors that contribute to someone's size. What we eat and how much we move accounts for less than 10%.

Learning all this left me desperate for answers – the same answers that Jacinta wanted so she could support Billie. Why are we so hell-bent on making folks smaller? Why are we panicking about a health epidemic where there isn't one? Why are so many teens being diagnosed with eating disorders but there are scant few headlines about it? Why do we automatically think bigger people should lose weight in order to support their health when we know health behaviours can improve health regardless of size?

If you have put your own child on a diet or used weight as a measure of your child's health in the past, please don't fret or be hard on yourself. You've been doing the absolute best you could with the information you've had. You are about to find the final piece of the 'I should control my child's weight' puzzle.

CHAPTER 8

Why are we so bothered by fat?

Let me tell you about a fiftieth birthday party I attended a couple of years ago. Around a table set with all manner of delicious celebratory foods sat a dozen or so remarkable women. Among us were self-made millionaires, authors, lawyers, Olympians, business owners, engineers, artists, mothers. I had known some of them for decades, which meant I had a sense of belonging and connection I don't often feel. The giggling and bubbles flowed easily and abundantly. It was a beautiful, love-filled afternoon.

At one point, though, that thing happened that often happens when a group of women gather together.

'I may as well just slap this cheesecake straight onto my thighs.'

'Oh, I'm being so naughty!'

'Why is the best food the hardest to resist?'

'If I don't stop now, I'll be rolling home.'

'I'm starting a fast on Monday.'

'Oh, I hate that you can eat all this and still look amazing.' (This was directed at the thinnest person in the room.)

I was the only one not laughing. In fact, I was inwardly cringing. My friends had contributed so much to the world, and yet here they were, unable to fully enjoy the food in front of them without apologising for their appetite or their size. What were they scared of? Becoming fat and announcing to the world their personal failing or moral weakness? Did they subconsciously understand that fat people have a much harder time in the world, and were voicing their fear of that happening to them? Collectively, that conversation was conveying a fearful sentiment and proclaiming our commitment out loud: *We must do all we can to not be a fat person.* But I would bet my house on the fact that if a properly fat person had been in the room, no one would have the stones to look them in the eye and say, 'I really don't want to look like you. I find it so unappealing, in fact, that I make my desire not to look like you clear to the world.'

Having an almost out-of-body experience, I sat there at the table, imagining younger generations looking back on this type of communal anti-fatness and drawing a direct line between social acceptance of body-centred self-deprecation and the perpetuation of size stigma and discrimination. Our generation is so steeped in it, we just can't see it.

As I sat there, the initial self-deprecating jibes turned into an outright discussion of what we should and shouldn't be eating, and how to get rid of the (obviously disgusting) kilos we might be putting on by indulging in the feast we were having. Please remember, we were not a group of teenagers being unduly influenced by an impossibly thin TikToker. We were a group of smart, successful women in our late forties to early sixties, all certain that our appetites and bodies needed taming. It's little wonder, then, that the pressure parents feel to help their children avoid fatness is intense.

If in the past you have tried to help your child lose weight or simply 'not get too big', you were probably doing so, at least in part, to help them avoid the pain of being a bigger person in a culture that is persistently mean to bigger people – just like Miranda, mother of eight-year-old Jona, tried to do.

Over several conversations, Miranda told me with sadness that she didn't see any alternative to encouraging Jona to lose weight because that had been the only path she had ever set for herself. She realised that she had believed it was okay to destroy her relationship with her body in an effort to achieve the body she was 'meant' to have: 'Like my size was the badge of my commitment to health, and I thought it could be the badge of Jona's commitment too.'

Miranda told me that she tried to lose weight because she wanted people to see that she was a 'good person'. She asked if I was familiar with what she described as the unspoken rules of weight loss: 'Eat as little as you possibly can; wrestle against your appetites and desires even when it ends in frustration and shame; express constant dissatisfaction with your body; attach your sense of self-worth to the external rewards reaped from how you look; when you succeed in losing weight, believe it's attributable to your hard work and judge others when they fail.'

I knew them intimately. Maybe you do too.

'Did dieting work?' I asked.

'No question,' she said, 'until I stopped and the weight returned and then some. But I still nudged my bright, energetic boy towards dieting, so that he could avoid being bigger than I believed he should be. I'm so glad I can now see it for what it is – utter madness!'

When thinking about why we are so driven to avoid being fat, and why that shows that we're 'good people', I can't help thinking about the messages I got when I was growing up. Of course, there were blatant 'obesity epidemic' messages, but there were many more subtle ways that the idea of being fat was presented as a bad thing.

I grew up in Wellington in the 1970s and 1980s. My parents were fine people. They were loving and encouraging and believed, for the most part, in social justice. Both my parents were feminists, encouraging my sister and me to become whatever we wanted to be, and to not let glass ceilings stop us. We talked about gay marriage and combating racism. We were taught to believe that everyone deserves respect and equal access to resources.

That value was applicable to all groups of people, except for one. I bet you can guess which group wasn't afforded the same respect as others. It was fine in my family to laugh at fat jokes. Or to be annoyed at someone taking up too much space in an aeroplane seat. The overarching message was that fat people really should sort themselves out before heading into public and inconveniencing everyone else.

The only time I remember my mother bad-mouthing anyone behind their back was when she couldn't understand why a particular person didn't lose some weight. 'It's so bad for their health! They'll feel terrible at the beach this year!'

Needless to say, all my role models at the time were thin. Olivia Newton-John in her shiny black leggings. Bo Derek on the beach. Tina Turner. Sinéad O'Connor. Debbie Harry. All slim.

Plus, my parents were dieters. By the time I was 12, I knew all the dieting terminology. *Good days* and *bad days. Slimming food* and *fattening food. Weight Watchers. Pritikin. Atkins. Weigh-ins.* While all those terms and diets are out of fashion now, I imagine most 12-year-olds would know the more current terminology. *Keto. Paleo. Detoxing. Low carb. Counting macros. Intermittent fasting.*

Up until the age of 13, I didn't think any of those things related to me at all. I was as skinny as a stick and had heard the comments about my body: 'What I wouldn't do to look like that again! Oh, she could wear anything! Legs up to her armpits!' I knew I had the kind of body you were meant to have, even if nobody had ever said that outright to me. It was expected that I would grow into an adult who looked like my paternal grandmother: not much taller than I was at 13 and only a few kilos heavier.

But that's not what happened. When puberty struck, it was like someone put a bicycle pump in my mouth and – *oooof* – I blew up overnight. Stretch marks unfurled all over my body. I was horrified. And terrified. I knew one thing for certain: it was my job to make sure I got back to how I used to look.

So I did what I'd been trained my whole life to do: I ate as little as I could and exercised as much as I possibly could. It was then that my eating disorder kicked in.

I'm not trying to get anyone to stop dieting. By all means, feel free to engage in weight loss if you want. I think you should be able to do so without any judgement or ridicule from anyone; I'm staunch about that. What I'm saying is that the evidence suggests this route is unlikely to bring you or your loved ones lasting satisfaction, thinness, health or joy.

My belief is that while we focus on foregoing the delights of our palates in order to be thinner, our bodies are stuck in survival mode waiting for the starvation to stop, desperately wanting to live in a more satisfying and peaceful way. But that's only half the problem. When we are busy attempting to be 'not fat', we distract ourselves from a far bigger, more sinister problem: the way anti-fat bias is harming our culture and everyone who lives in it.

What is anti-fat bias?

The term 'anti-fat bias' refers to our collective ideas about fatness and health that aren't based on anything other than negative assumptions and beliefs. Until we are willing to acknowledge them and make changes, we are going to stay stuck.

In order to recognise anti-fat bias in ourselves, it's helpful to shine light on situations where anti-fatness manifests itself – in places we might not have previously noticed. With awareness, you can consciously decide to stop buying into anti-fatness or unintentionally promoting it. You can look at your values and make an informed decision, rather than blindly forging ahead and not realising the impact you're having.

Fundamentally, anti-fat bias is a belief that being fat is inferior and that being thinner is superior. It's believing that fatness is morally bad (*they shouldn't have let themselves go!*). And not only is it morally bad, it should be eradicated (*the war on obesity!*). It should be eradicated not just for 'health' reasons, but because fat people are lazy, less attractive and not as smart or as nice as thinner folks and they cost the country more.

When we are raising our children with those beliefs in the background, how can we possibly be okay with them putting on weight?

Let's look at each one of those beliefs and see if they stack up in reality. Are fat people lazy? Is it really possible that fat tissue affects someone's motivation? If it's the fatness that makes someone lazy then if they lost weight, they would no longer be lazy. It would also mean that if fatness caused laziness, we could tell instantly the extent of someone's laziness by their size. I would be a bit lazier than someone who wears a size down from me and a bit less lazy than someone who wears a size up. If that were true, all we'd need to know about someone being a hard worker is their pant size. No need for a 360-degree evaluation at work. It would also mean we'd never find a lazy thin person.

I have swung between six dress sizes over my lifetime. I wasn't a jot lazier at my biggest than I was at my smallest. If anything, I was lazier at my smallest, because I had less energy. In case you weren't aware, very fat people have become surgeons, professors, prime ministers; they've written books, mothered children, run schools, run marathons, won scholarships, chaired boards, become monks, captained ships, led dance troupes, directed movies, led sports teams. Laziness has no place in any of those positions.

I'm not suggesting that being fat means you're *not* lazy. I'm saying that we can't assume. Again, to hammer home the point, we can't jump to conclusions about people based on the way they look.

But aren't fat folks lazy when it comes to health? As we touched on earlier, by the age of 45 the average British woman has tried 61 diets. Most people who embark on diets tend to be on the larger end of the size scale. Doing something as hard as dieting over and over again is the antithesis of laziness. It shows dedication and commitment.

Sometimes the 'cost' of obesity is used to insinuate that bigger people shouldn't allow themselves to get so fat and cost the rest of us so much money. But if we are so concerned about costs due to perceived preventable conditions, why are we not just as het up about the cost of sports injuries, family violence or drinking, when those things are demonstrably more preventable? All those sports players who just can't be bothered to keep themselves in proper shape so they don't get injured – why don't we call them lazy? Why do we have wine awards and allow our drinking culture to go on almost unchecked when the cost to the country outstrips the revenue alcohol brings in by $6.657 billion? Why are we not asking sports players and drinkers to consider the cost to the rest

Many academics
argue that our collective
health would increase
if our systems stopped
stigmatising fat people and
prescribing weight loss.

of us, and instead lay that particular complaint solely at fat people's doors?

The assumptions that fat people are lazy is the reason why fat folks are paid less and are underrepresented in management positions.

Let's talk about healthcare more broadly, and how we very rarely hear about the systemic issues and attitudes that prevent bigger folks from receiving good healthcare. Instead, we focus on the cost of obesity as a personal responsibility issue.

Here's the shameful truth: if I, as a thin person, go to a health professional with, say, a sore knee, I will get my knee problem attended to. I'll get scanned and offered strengthening exercises or surgery or appropriate stretching. I'll get treated with care and concern.

If a fatter person goes with the same complaint, the likelihood of being offered such care and concern is far lower. They are likely to be told that fat is their problem before any tests are done (even though there is no evidence that weight loss makes a difference to joint pain). Sometimes patients are told not to return unless they lose weight. That means a muscle imbalance, ligament strain or meniscus tear can be left undiagnosed. All of which will remain problematic, regardless of weight loss.

This is because fat people often face prejudice and stigmatisation from healthcare providers. Yet it's fatness and lack of personal responsibility that are most often blamed for poor health in larger people, not poor care received due to anti-fat bias. Many academics argue that our collective health would increase if our systems stopped stigmatising fat people and prescribing weight loss.

The thing that feels so fundamentally frustrating about this is that instead of measuring fatness – with the BMI and the poor quality of information it gives us about an individual's health – it is entirely possible to measure any number of other factors: we can take people's blood pressure and resting heart rate, and do blood work. We can ask people about their diet and exercise habits (and train healthcare providers to believe what patients tell them), and we can look at the history of heart disease in families and discuss that. We can order scans and take tests.

In other words, it is possible to get a good picture of someone's health without talking about fatness at all. If someone's resting heart rate is too fast, we know that some sustained exercise each day can make a difference regardless of what someone weighs. If someone has high blood pressure, we can talk about exercise and nutrition and medication.

Also, in case you haven't considered the idea before, weight is a characteristic, not a behaviour. I only bring it up because weight and smoking are often used as examples when it comes to developing good habits and breaking bad ones. Sometimes these habit-forming ideas are fabulous, but certain contemporary self-improvement authors seem unable to understand that weight is not a habit.

The advice might sound like this: 'If you are serious about your weight, a great way to start is by avoiding certain aisles at the supermarket. Fresh whole foods are on the outer ring of the supermarket, so keeping to those aisles can help you to eat whole foods more regularly and avoid processed foods.'

Can you see what they have done here? They are suggesting that weight is a behaviour, instead of being very clear that eating healthy food is a habit, and weight is a complex result of many things. Habits are things we can 'do'. Things like daily exercise, eating greens and drinking water. Sleep is a habit. But your weight is no more a habit than blonde hair.

The problem, of course, is that we live in an era where a straight line has been drawn between engaging in health-promoting habits and having a certain body size. There's an assumption that if we get into the habits of regular exercise and eating veggies, a body characteristic will automatically follow. As you learned in the previous chapter, this notion is unfounded. It's our collective stories and assumptions about fatness – AKA anti-fat bias – that keep this idea alive.

Anti-fat bias is learned far younger than you might think. Research shows that kids as young as three already believe that fat is bad and thin is good. At five years old we already have anti-fat bias baked into us.

By five, kids have already seen the idea of 'size' constantly associated with negative traits. Beloved children's author Roald Dahl repeatedly used fatness as a signpost for ugliness and meanness. Dudley, Harry Potter's horrible cousin, has his fatness linked directly to his ugliness, stupidity, malice, laziness, greediness and self-centeredness. He embodies the predictable fat trope. This trope can be seen again and again in kids' movies, books and television shows – and in movies and media for all ages. We see fat people portrayed as losers or villains again and again: Austin Powers's Fat Bastard is gluttonous and crude; Ursula from *The Little Mermaid* is manipulative and cruel; and when Monica from *Friends* was 'Fat Monica' she was pathetic and food-obsessed. Now that you've seen anti-fat bias, you may not be able to unsee it. I imagine you'll start to notice it everywhere, because it is everywhere.

Other ways anti-fatness plays out in popular culture

The argument that fatness equals poor morality comes from the reality that higher weight is correlated with many health issues. As we've discussed at length, body size is often (without good evidence) blamed for health problems, and failure to lose weight is also blamed on the individual (again without evidence). These things added together lead to the belief that fat is a personal failing.

And if fatness is an individual failure, the fatness of kids is a parenting failure. Nothing demonstrates this more clearly than when parents have their children taken from them for being too big.

In a 2021 UK court case, two teenagers were removed from loving parents because the parents had failed to make them lose weight. The two teenagers were taken into care over their failure to shed pounds, turn up to Weight Watchers meetings or submit Fitbit information to Social Services. Because of this, a judge ruled that they must live with a foster family because otherwise 'they will continue to put on weight'.

In an interview about the case, the judge said: 'The case was such an unusual one because the children had clearly had some very good parenting, as they were polite, bright and engaging.'

If taking well-raised kids from loving parents on the basis of them being 'too fat' isn't a sign of systemic anti-fatness and a signal that keeping kids from gaining weight is one of a parent's most important roles, I don't know what is.

As parents, how do we raise a child who is fat or might become fat to have a good life in a culture like that? Up until now, many of us have done our best to prevent our kids from becoming fat. We are *told* to do that and we know that if we fail, the worst-case scenario is that we have our kids taken from us. No wonder we are worried and frustrated.

Diversity in Western culture has rightfully gained more attention over the last few years. It's not uncommon in this day and age for businesses to have performance measures centred on inclusion and diversity. However, a 2019 Harvard study shows that although we are making some progress when it comes to biases and stigma against marginalised folks, one area is lagging. While other forms of stigma (for example, racism, sexism, homophobia) have experienced a shift in cultural self-awareness and subsequently a decrease in impact on individuals, the study shows the only form of cultural stigma that has grown significantly in the last 20 years is anti-fat bias.

But anti-fatness is not a new phenomenon. It was around as far back as the 1600s. Sabrina Strings, a professor of sociology at the University of California, has traced the roots of anti-fatness and studied its racial origins. The argument against fatness back in the seventeenth century was that it was associated too closely with Black people. If white people wanted to remain superior, they would do well to make sure they didn't put on weight. In other words, anti-fatness has been around a long time and has racist roots.

The cost of anti-fat bias for kids

So how does this entrenched anti-fat bias affect our kids? Fat kids will often poke fun at themselves about being fat, or play along with the joke, only to later go to a private place and eat for comfort, not knowing who they can talk to or really understanding why they feel that way, knowing only that their body is wrong, they are somehow at fault and that they must go along with the idea that their body is funny in order to survive.

In schools, size bullying is the most common form of bullying, yet it's the form of bullying that schools are least likely to do anything about. The cultural idea that those kids 'had it coming' and perhaps 'a bit of tough love wouldn't go astray' is at play. This again sends the message that fatness is the individual's problem, and that if they are encountering bullying, they would do well to sort their body out so that others are not compelled to harm them because of it. This kind of thinking is eerily similar to the idea that women 'provoke' sexual abuse and that if women could dress appropriately, then men wouldn't be led on, and sexual abuse wouldn't be such a problem.

Most of us accept that it is not okay to bully someone for the colour of their skin or a physical disability. We would never tell someone on the receiving end of such abuse to change their physical characteristics or behaviour to be more acceptable to the bully and society. So why is it acceptable to think, *Oh well, if the fat kid lost weight, they could stop this from happening*?

It's amazing how often parents are blamed in this scenario as well. I've been in earshot of a mum saying, 'If their parents didn't feed them McDonald's and allow junk food at home, they wouldn't be treated so badly at school.'

Anti-fatness culture also demands that kids try to lose weight. I have heard 14-year-olds say they'd rather be thin than do well at school. I have seen five-year-olds swapping dieting tips. And in New Zealand, four out of five teenage girls think sport is hard to participate in because they feel judged about their body. One of the most common concerns I hear from parents is that their child won't swim with their friends because they don't want to be seen in togs.

Eating disorder services in New Zealand are stretched beyond capacity. Anorexia nervosa is the third most common chronic disorder affecting adolescent girls, with the second highest mortality rate of all psychiatric disorders.

These are not simply childhood issues that most people will grow out of. A survey conducted by *Glamour* magazine said that 97% of women have an 'I hate my body' moment every single day.

But why does anti-fatness persist so stubbornly?

Again, this is a huge question that has many complicated answers. Indeed it could be a book in itself and even that would leave threads hanging. But for now, I want to focus on the huge commercial viability of the promise of weight loss. There is a massive financial incentive to turning a blind eye to the fact that weight loss has been categorically shown to not work for the vast majority of people, and that it comes with the potential for a great deal of harm.

Everyone from Big Pharma with their weight-loss drugs and weight-loss surgeries through to reality TV shows showcasing weight loss, to individual Instagram influencers who sell exercise programmes and lifestyle changes that promise to flatten your tummy or help you shed menopausal weight gain or sort out pretty much any weight-gain scenario – they all stand to gain from anti-fat bias. Even if the main driver of what someone is selling is health but losing weight is sold as an added bonus, a financial gain is being made from the unsubstantiated promise that your body will change if you follow their advice.

The reality is that anti-fat bias is far-reaching, stubborn and financially lucrative. The global business of weight loss as part of the wellness industry is valued around $USD1.5 trillion. That is a massive flywheel that will take something extraordinary to slow down, let alone stop.

It's no wonder that we parents want to protect our kids from fatness. Not only do the parenting messages about not letting your precious child get 'too fat' come thick and fast, but the world out there is brutal to fat people. As parents wanting to protect our kids from harm, it makes perfect sense to fear it.

The hidden challenge

This brings us to the hidden challenge. In Section One, I said there was a hidden challenge behind our struggle as parents when it comes to allowing our children to eat what is right for them. What I didn't mention was how high the stakes are when we fail to acknowledge it. The hidden challenge is this: when you decide not to buy into anti-fat bias and to let your child's weight land where it falls, you will come smack-up against society's deeply entrenched anti-fat beliefs. Even though there is strong evidence that letting go of trying to control your child's weight leads to better long-term health outcomes, standing up to those anti-fat beliefs requires uncommon courage.

When I first told friends I was done with dieting and trying to control my weight, and not only that, that I was actively advocating for the rights of all-sized people to be treated with respect, I was met with much scorn. Smart folks became incensed and discussions quickly broke down into 'let's agree to disagree' territory. I was amazed how little sway the science and data and my lived experience had. The anti-fatness I encountered was as stubborn as it was emotionally charged.

The knowledge you've just gained in this section empowered my client Miranda to focus on things that could potentially contribute to her son Jona's long-term health, while being aware of anti-fat bias and doing her best to avoid it. Miranda learned that she could encourage her son to eat veggies and do exercise (without wanting him to do either for size management). She could help Jona to see the injustice faced in our culture by people with bodies that are bigger, and to let go of any residual feeling that it was Jona's responsibility to keep himself a certain weight. Miranda could teach Jona to stand up for himself at school and at the doctor's office, asserting his right to be treated with respect and dignity and get access to good healthcare without being shamed or told his body was wrong.

Like me, she noticed a lot of pushback from friends and family who were confronted by her new approach. Her decision to stop all attempts at changing Jona's body size, and indeed to embrace the idea that larger-bodied people are worthy of the same respect and access to resources as their thinner contemporaries, was met with resistance. Hackles were raised. Anger aroused. Attempts to turn the conversation back towards Jona's responsibility and 'concern for health' were earnest and sincere.

This resistance from others, if you encounter it, can make you feel lonely and vulnerable – not surprising, given that the act of embracing body size is also an act of cultural change. Endeavouring to make cultural change can feel isolating because it shines a light on the unearned benefits bestowed on some members of society.

And those who have the most to gain from those benefits – those who are seen as morally or socially superior, or who are financially rewarded for selling weight-management services and products – can feel angry and resentful and focus those emotions on you. History tells us that when those who are oppressed stand up for themselves, they are seen as 'angry' or 'hysterical', and their arguments are ridiculed. Those who are allies to the oppressed often find themselves shut out of social circles where they used to be included. So if you

Refusing to apologise for the size of our kids' bodies is a radical and powerful act.

have the stones to stand up to the current system, which oppresses bigger people, that is testament to your bravery indeed.

Miranda described this cultural change beautifully: 'I've gone from a "good fat person", who was showing the world they were doing all the things they were "supposed" to be doing to make my body acceptable, to someone who chooses to see her body as something to cherish, respect and care for.'

This reminds me of a brilliant line from Michael Hobbs in the podcast *Maintenance Phase*: 'Coming out as gay isn't about being willing to tell the world you are homosexual, it's about telling the world you will no longer apologise for being gay.' Refusing to apologise for our kids' body size is a radical and powerful act.

While practising body acceptance is more likely to lead to better health outcomes for our children, not to mention inner satisfaction and peace for them, it may also bring them (and you) outer conflict. As a parent, this choice is amplified because it gets overlaid with judgement about 'bad parenting' and even greater 'health concerns'.

Part of my motivation for writing this book is to help those conversations become less combative and less emotionally charged. Once enough people have this knowledge, there will be a sea change. But for that to happen, some of us have to go first.

Reading this book, you might imagine that I would refuse to associate with anyone who disagrees with me about weight and fatness and bodies. That is not the case. If I demanded everyone consider food and bodies and anti-fat bias the way I do in order for us to have a good relationship, I wouldn't be on speaking terms with some people I love.

Why don't I need others to share my perspective on this topic? I believe, first and foremost, in body autonomy. That means I believe that every one of us should be free to eat however we want, without judgement from others. If someone wants to pursue weight loss or eat a particular way, I have no problem with that. That doesn't mean I stay silent when I notice someone's body autonomy being disrespected or opinions about fatness being presented as fact. I attempt to speak up with the goal of sharing what I've learned, with the intention of making the world a kinder, more inclusive place based on the evidence we have at hand. When my opinion is unwelcome or ridiculed, I attempt to do what I hope others would do for me: respect our differences. The last thing I want to do is create more division in an already divided world.

In the next chapter, we'll look at one of the most significant things we can do to demonstrate positive change in the way we see bodies, so that our culture might follow. Our entire culture is unlikely to change overnight. Anti-fat bias may not be eradicated in our lifetime. But we can have an impact on how bodies are talked about, presented and viewed in our immediate environment. We can make considerable and unapologetic changes in our homes, in the way we speak and in the parenting rules we employ. We're about to get practical.

CHAPTER 9

Environment matters

Now that you've learned that fatness isn't related to health in the way you may have thought it was, and you can see the cultural bias underpinning many of our collective beliefs, you may find yourself in a couple of places. Maybe you are dwelling in the hopelessness of it all. I certainly did. I moped and fretted and felt powerless. I'd love for you to get that fretting and moping out of the way quickly, though, so you can get down to the business of helping your child have a healthier relationship with food and their body. Or maybe you are fired up and ready to act. Or perhaps you don't want to think about it too much; you just want some guidance as to what to do next.

Wherever you are, it helps to have concrete actions you can take, so this chapter is about getting you into action.

Specifically, I'm going to offer you practical steps you can take in your home, in your community and in your life, to help you raise your children to have a healthy relationship with food and feel good in their bodies. These steps are designed to create an environment where all bodies are seen as good bodies, regardless of how they look. And everyone has a body, so that affects a lot of people. Sounds good, right?

Get rid of anti-fat messages where you can

I'm going to start with a practice that you can do for yourself and, in the process, teach your children to do the same. As parents it's great to do these things for yourself so you're not sending the message 'do as I say, not as I do'. Eating disorder dietitian Marcia Evans says that eliminating anti-fat messages from your environment, wherever you can, is one of the most powerful and positive actions we can take for affecting body image for everyone. And it's as simple as it is effective.

It's basically a matter of decluttering anti-fat messages from your physical and online environments. That means you get rid of books, magazines and images in your home that send the message that fat is bad and thin is good.

Pay particular attention to recipe books that promise to make you look a certain way if you follow a certain way of eating. Begin to repopulate your home with images that show a diverse range of bodies. You could buy a coffee-table book with a fat yoga instructor on the front. Seek out novels where the hero goes against the stereotypes – a love interest with a disability, for example.

Judith, one of my clients, told me that she had stuck a sticky note with her weight-loss goals on her bathroom mirror, so in the decluttering process, she took them down and threw them away. She replaced the weight-loss goals with the goal of running a marathon, and next to this she stuck up a picture of a fat woman crossing the finish line. She wanted to be reminded that having the energy to move and do challenging things was what she actually wanted, regardless of her body size. What inspired her the most was thinking about demonstrating to her three children that body size and shape didn't have to be a barrier to a happy and fulfilling life.

If you have weight-loss goals displayed in a prominent place, I encourage you to move them out of your child's view and to refrain from discussing your goals or your journey within their earshot. You could consider taking a leaf out of Judith's book and think about your goal. Is it feeling good in your clothes? Having more energy? Doing something physically challenging with your body? All of those are possible without your size changing. Talk about those goals with your family. Find an image of someone achieving your goal who has a body that resembles your current size.

Once you've decluttered your physical spaces, do the same with your online spaces. Get into the weeds of your social media and unfollow any accounts that promote the idea that thinner is better. If you think an online account encourages larger folks (or indeed anyone) to be smaller, or sends the message that larger folk should be doing something to make themselves smaller, or that larger folks are inferior in any way to thinner ones, axe it from your feeds. If you can't quite put your finger on it, but you get a sense that unapologetically larger folks would not be welcome, trust your instinct and unfollow.

Watch out for accounts that dress themselves up as being health-related but actually use weight loss as a measure of success – for example, accounts that promise to help you overcome emotional eating and drop a dress size in the process. It is perfectly possible at any size to eat without stressing or overthinking or feeling ashamed, and there is no evidence that weight loss is guaranteed to occur if you do. Of course, you might lose weight, but you also might not.

If you are in menopause or the menopause transition, keep your eyes peeled for accounts run by thin 50-something women who claim to help with weight management. Humans tend to get fatter as we age. Putting on weight is a natural and healthy part of the ageing process. Promising you can have your pre-menopausal body back is like promising a teen they can get back to their pre-pubescent size. Again, there are no studies that support long-term weight loss at menopause or other times of life, and the dangers of triggering an eating disorder remain high (menopausal women are the second largest at-risk group of developing an eating disorder after teenaged girls). That's not to say there are no nutritional or physical things we can do that make a menopausal body feel better, we just can't guarantee a particular body size if we do those things. Besides, modelling acceptance of our changing body is great for our kids.

As you practise decluttering, think about the impact this can have on your family and how it can influence the way you parent. You could begin by getting your family involved in the process. Make a game of it. Get them to help you go through your magazines or recipe books and see if they can spot anti-fatness sooner than you can. Make it a stipulation of using the internet in your home that you don't follow businesses or influencers who promote anti-fatness.

Decluttering like this has two significant benefits. It means there are fewer anti-fat messages in the world. This means we are making the world a kinder place for fat people and we are less likely to consider being fat undesirable. It also means everyone in your family is likely to feel better about their body. When we are constantly reminded that certain bodies are good and certain ones are bad, we all suffer the consequence of feeling like our body isn't up to scratch. This decluttering, then, is good for us and our kids, personally and culturally.

Hide the scales

Once Judith had changed her weight-loss goals to performance goals, she hid her family scales. I suggest you do the same. Put them away and get them out only if you need to weigh a member of the family for medical reasons. If you keep the scales in a cupboard, your kids won't see scales as an important piece of equipment. It conveys the idea that weight isn't something we need to think about unless we need to know how much medicine to take, for example.

A second reason to put the scales away is that for many of us, the act of weighing ourselves can come with a high emotional charge. For years, the number on the scale literally dictated the kind of day

I would have. If your children see that a low number makes you feel good and a high number makes you feel bad, they will learn that weight is really, terribly important. But if you keep the scales in a cupboard and don't weigh yourself in front of the kids, they won't see any potential emotional fallout from the number on the scale.

If weighing yourself brings unwanted emotion and you'd like your weight to have less of an emotional charge, simply stop weighing yourself. People can experience a huge sense of liberation when they stop using the external value of weight as a driver for their inner sense of value.

It is far easier to tune into what your body does for you and feel appreciative of it when we are not distracted by how much it does or doesn't weigh. Demonstrating to your kids that you don't weigh-in adds to an environment that is inclusive of all-sized people.

Remember, you can decline to be weighed at the doctor's surgery. If it's absolutely necessary to be weighed, please know that you are entitled to ask that your weight not be told to you. If you are pressured or encouraged to be weighed for any other reason, you can ask that it be recorded in your notes that you don't want to be weighed because it causes you emotional stress but that you received pressure to do so.

You can also ask your doctor to avoid discussing weight with your child. Request that if your healthcare provider has concerns about weight, they talk to you in private where your child can't hear. Be clear that it's okay to talk about improving fitness, blood pressure or blood sugars but not to use weight as a measure of success for those things.

It's no joke

Let's talk about fat jokes. Fat jokes come in many different guises. While you'll be able to spot the glaringly obvious ones, be extra vigilant about jokes that suggest weight gain or fatness is synonymous with unattractiveness.

Take the 2019 film *Isn't It Romantic* as an example. Rebel Wilson's character, Natalie, a lifelong cynic when it comes to romantic comedies, finds herself in an alternate universe where she's the leading lady in her own romantic comedy. When she gains weight in this world, her love interest loses interest, only for it to rekindle when she loses the weight again.

It's noteworthy that Natalie's size is the only thing that changes in her love interest's perception. She's still a smart, kind-hearted architect. Listening to the dialogue through an anti-fat lens is difficult. When my kids asked why I was shouting at the TV, it sparked some great conversations.

So what can we do when we hear fat jokes or see them in the media? Make fat jokes unacceptable in your home, and bring attention to them when they pop up. Imagine your child cracking blatantly racist, homophobic or sexist jokes. Would you find them funny? Would they fit with the values of your household? Would you let them slide, or would you use them as a learning opportunity for your child? I suggest you treat fat jokes exactly the same way.

Remember, in the same way that stereotyping and cracking derogatory jokes about race or gender harms all of us, making derogatory jokes about bigger-bodied people does too. When your children hear adults laughing at jokes about fat people, they receive a very clear message that fat is something to avoid at all costs. *Look at the ridicule you get!*

When children hear others making or laughing at fat jokes without consequence, it can be taken as a licence to be mean to larger kids at school. If they hear adults making those jokes then why wouldn't it be okay to make fun of fat people themselves?

I get how awkward it can feel to stand up for something that you have previously not noticed. You might get told you're over-reacting, that you're nitpicking or being stupid. But isn't that what always happens to people who are willing to cause social change? It's up to each of us to decide if we are going to be part of that change or wait for others to go first.

Stereotypes to watch for

In the last chapter we touched on the idea that before our kids reach school age, it's likely they have already decided that being fat is bad. In preschool, kids are not connecting fat with health. But they are connecting weight with being mean, lazy, happy, smart, popular and beautiful. This is one of the reasons why it's so important to call out stereotypes to our kids. It's also a great argument for not talking about health and weight to kids in educational settings.

In our family, we have had many discussions about why fatness is always so fundamentally linked to greediness. And why it is that only bigger kids are deemed to have insatiable appetites, when many kids love cookies and eat a lot, regardless of their size. Why bigger kids are rarely shown as cool, or popular, or attractive. Why we are never invited to be envious of a fat kid. Why the princess is almost always thin (unless she is awful). Why villains are a mixture of thin and fat, but it's rare indeed to find a fat heroine. Why larger folks are almost always the loser, the unkempt, the not-so-smart one.

Of course, there are exceptions to these rules. There are outliers we can point to and feel better about ourselves and our culture, but I'm going to suggest you guard against using the exceptions as evidence that fat stereotypes are a thing of the past and pay attention to the dominant narratives. By all means, celebrate the exceptions! But don't confuse them with the reality that the lion's share of kids' (and adults') movies and books show fatness in a very poor light. Otherwise, why would kids as young as three – as Phebe Cramer and Tiffany Steinwert point out in their research – believe that fatness is so bad? No one is born with that belief. It is learned.

If anti-fatness can be learned, it can also be unlearned. The very first step in that process is to acknowledge it. Make your kids aware of what's going on. Teach them that we don't have to buy into it. We have a choice. We can choose to stand up to it.

Once you start to see fat-shaming in kids' media, you'll start to see it everywhere. When you do, you can make it a game for your family – simply say 'Stereotype!' and start a discussion. We can seek out books for ourselves and our kids that portray characters that don't fit the stereotypes (see resources on page 281).

Terms that medicalise and stigmatise

When I was a tween, my mother stopped using the word 'ladies' and opted for 'women' instead. She taught us to never say the word 'Maoris' because te reo doesn't have an 's' in it; putting that 's' where it doesn't belong, she told us, was disrespectful. It was absolutely unacceptable in our house to use 'gay' as a derogatory term. Living in an environment where I was encouraged to think about the impact the words we use have on others gave me a conscious experience of the impact that words have on us individually and culturally.

Perhaps that focus on language and the power of words is in part why I'm so keen to see our culture change the current terms we use when talking about fatness. As you read the words and terms that I suggest you avoid from here on in, imagine how doing so is helping to transform our anti-fat environment and make the world better for everyone.

The specific words I suggest you stop using are:

- ***Obese/obesity.*** These terms medicalise fatness. It is impossible to use the term 'obesity' without connotations of sick or unhealthy fatness. Instead, say 'fat' or 'bigger bodied'. 'Fat' is the term many fat people are asking the world to use. When the word 'fat' becomes a simple descriptor, the idea that fat is derogatory loses its power. If you need to describe someone's body size, I suggest you ask them what term they would like you to use. Don't call an individual fat unless they have asked you to.

- ***Overweight.*** Over which weight? We don't say normal height, overheight or underheight. So why do we do this with weight or size? Notice how 'thin', 'average' and 'fat' simply describe (without medicalising), and also notice how 'underweight', 'normal' and 'overweight' makes it feel like there is only one correct weight to be.
- ***Healthy weight.*** This term in particular grinds my gears. If we know that there are some fat people with normal blood pressure and a good resting heart rate, who eat a diet rich in variety and nutrition and get regular exercise – that is, they are healthy – and we know there are some medium-sized people who have high blood pressure, an elevated heart rate, eat a diet low in nutrition and get very little exercise, then why is the medium-sized person a 'healthy' weight and the fat person an 'unhealthy' weight? It makes no sense. Let's stop using the term 'healthy weight' and stick to simple descriptors.
- ***Ideal weight.*** This is even worse, isn't it? Using the word 'ideal' coupled with someone's weight is just sending all the wrong messages. Would we ever congratulate someone for being the ideal colour? So let's not do it with size.
- ***BMI.*** As we've seen, the BMI was never intended to be used as an individual health measure. And yet the language used in BMI tables helps to solidify the idea that 'healthy weight', 'overweight' and 'obese' are meaningful health measures when clearly they are not.

If we want kids to hear messages other than 'your body needs to look a certain way', we need to be the ones who offer an alternative point of view. One way we can do that with our families is to practise gratitude for our bodies.

- ***The obesity epidemic.*** If we stop using the word obesity, we will automatically stop using the term 'obesity epidemic', but I've put it here to suggest that when you hear this term, you should consciously question the messages accompanying the term, rather than blindly believe them. Ask yourself, where does this idea come from? Whose interest is this promoting? Who funded this research?

Shifting the focus from how bodies look to what they do

It's not often that a body is talked about as a gift, a tool or a mechanism for the express purpose of experiencing this magical thing called life. It is rare for kids to be party to conversations about how the body we have is the only one we've got, so treating it with dignity and respect is a great idea. The emphasis on changing it to be better, specifically to look better, is a more prevalent idea.

This means that if we want kids to hear messages other than 'your body needs to look a certain way', we need to be the ones who offer an alternative point of view. One way we can do that with our families is to practise gratitude for our bodies.

Practising gratitude has been shown to make us feel calmer, happier, more content and less angry. As Johann Hari tells us in his book *Lost Connections*, gratitude has a powerful positive effect on mental health. Shifting our kids' focus from what their body looks like to what their body does helps them shift their focus from external to internal values. When we have a stronger sense of internal value than external value, we are less susceptible to the powerful influence of anti-fat beliefs.

Here are some ways you and your family can include practising gratitude for your bodies into your daily routine.

Bedtime gratitude

For kids up to around nine years of age, you can incorporate a gratitude meditation into their bedtime routine. You'll find a link to a printable script, with directions on how to use it, on page 281. For parents with young kids, this bedtime routine can become one of the best parts of the day. I smile at the funny things parents tell me their kids say: 'Mum, Mum, Mum! Can we please thank our eyebrows? What about our farts?'

If your child is a bit older, you could suggest they do the meditation for themselves. If they are at a stage of thinking absolutely everything you suggest is something to avoid entirely, you could just tell them it's something you are doing and ask them what they think about it. You'll find some ways to have conversations about this kind of thing in the next section, so the conversation doesn't end with them rolling their eyes and walking away.

Play gratitude games

If you have younger kids, or your family is open to word games in the car or at the table, you can get playful with ideas about gratitude.

Here's one way to set it up. Someone could start off by saying, 'I'm grateful for my eyes because I get to see the people I love and I get to read.' Then it's the next person's turn, and so on.

You could also play a game called What Works Well? Take turns to each say one thing that works well about your bodies. It could be that your skin works well at being waterproof or stretchy. It could be that your eyelids are working well at blinking.

Curate their reading material

Add some books to your child's reading list to ensure they see a variety of different bodies being the hero of the story. Check out the links on page 281 for websites that list body-positive books for all ages.

Compliments and greetings

Take a moment to think about the most common compliments you hear in our culture. How many times a day do you hear people commenting on how someone looks? It might be that someone's looking lovely or their outfit is nice or their hair looks good or that they've lost weight. How often are children told they are 'gorgeous' or 'adorable' or 'cute'? Can you see how all of these greetings and compliments are praising their outward or aesthetic appearance?

Remember back in Section One when we talked about how children are figuring out their value in the world? If everyone keeps going on about how they look (and about how everyone else looks), they'll start connecting the dots. *How I look must be extremely important; it's usually the first comment people make!*

The good thing is that because compliments and greetings happen so regularly, they give us a chance to switch from external-value statements (*you look so cute!*) to using internal-value ones (*seeing you makes my day*). In this way, we can use compliments and greetings to shift our kids' focus from what they look like to who they are as a person. They also provide a fabulous and regular opportunity to boost kids' sense of belonging and significance.

On the next page, you'll find examples of greetings and compliments that encourage a sense of belonging and significance instead of praising aesthetic appearance. They also have the added bonus of not using weight or size as a compliment. By using compliments in this way, you can help shift the culture to be kinder to bigger people. This not only helps your child individually but helps create cultural change.

I encourage you to practise these greetings and compliments in private, because remembering to use them in the moment is way harder than knowing you should in theory. We are so conditioned in our culture to praise looks, it can feel awkward and uncomfortable to encourage internal values instead. In order to have them front of mind, practise them while driving alone in the car or doing the vacuuming – both are great opportunities to ensure you remember them when you need them.

To get you started, here is a list of non-appearance-based compliments and greetings that focus on a child's (or indeed anyone's) attributes, qualities and behaviours.

Greetings

Hello, it's so great to see you!

Seeing you has made my day!

I've been looking forward to seeing you.

Hey, how's that project you're working on going?

I'm always pleased to see you.

Your presence always lights up the room.

Great to see you, always full of life!

Great to meet you. I've heard a lot of lovely things about you.

Compliments

I admire your thoughtfulness.

You have such great energy!

Your smile is contagious!

I admire your passion for ______.

I love your sense of humour!

Your creativity is inspiring.

Wow, that was brave!

That was very kind, thank you.

That is a unique perspective.

I appreciate your honesty.

You are a great problem solver.

Your resilience is admirable.

Thank you for listening, I like talking with you.

Your ideas make me think – I really like that.

You're a great team player!

Complimenting appearance while focusing on ability rather than looks

What great shoes! I bet they are great for running in.

Those pockets look fabulous for collecting treasures.

That outfit you've put together reflects your amazing sense of style.

Before we move on, I want to highlight one of the dangers of complimenting children, or indeed anyone, on weight loss. Remember, intentional weight loss can come with serious, potentially life-threatening consequences, and it's impossible to know what health issues someone has by looking at them. When I was in the clutches of an eating disorder, the two compliments I received more than any other were implied in the way I was asked if I'd lost weight and told how healthy I looked. They fuelled my disease like nothing else. Those compliments validated the pain I was in and temporarily made the suffering seem worthwhile – and they made me believe I didn't need help. Was I really sick if people kept telling me I looked so healthy?

By refusing to comment on weight loss, you are also respecting the reality that body diversity exists and that human beings will always come in many different shapes and sizes. Plus, you'll be reinforcing the message that who people are on the inside is far more important than the size of the container they get about in.

Think about your decision to stop commenting on other people's bodies, complimenting how they look, mentioning their weight or even mentioning their appearance. It has far greater reach than simply reinforcing your child's external value. Imagine how good it would be to give energy to a cultural groundswell, how wonderful it would be if future generations believed all bodies are good bodies. Imagine a culture that believes if you've got a body, any type of body, you've already won the lottery. When that happens, an unhealthy relationship with food and body will be a thing of the past.

Start using your compliments and greetings today and start to notice what happens around you. You'll see the genuine smiles on your friends' faces when you tell them how nice it is to see them and you'll notice your kids' confidence start to rise when you remind them of how kind, or funny, or brave they are.

Focus on boosting internal value

In this section, we've been discussing how to create an environment that reduces exposure to anti-fat bias and why that's so important. Now let's finish by thinking again about where our kids get their sense of belonging and significance.

When our culture has such a pervasive belief that our size – an external value – is of great importance, it's easy for anyone living in that culture to start to hook their size to their sense of belonging and significance. One of the ways we can interrupt that belief is to help our kids hook their value to their internal qualities. This will:

- help them believe in themselves regardless of how closely they fit social beauty standards,

- help them focus on sustainable, long-term health behaviours,
- give them the confidence to stand up to social inequity,
- and give them a kinder society to live in.

Instead of trying to achieve the impossible and control your child's size, you can choose to loosen your grip and learn to trust that it's perfect for them. As you've seen, embracing the size they are can lead to better long-term health outcomes than trying to control their weight. With that in mind, the next section takes you on a deeper dive into many areas parents are concerned about.

Summary of Section Two

- A child's size does not indicate good or bad parenting.
- The BMI doesn't tell us anything about an individual's health, only relative fatness, and it does that poorly.
- Health and weight are separate. It is possible to improve health without seeing any change in weight.
- Weight loss is only sustainable in the long run for very few people. For the rest, it has many serious downsides.
- We can't make assumptions about a person's health or morality by looking at them.
- Our culture has a deep-seated bias against larger people that contributes to the health issues they face.

Parenting tips

- Stop focusing on how bodies look and start focusing on what they do.
- Practise body gratitude, either as a meditation before bed or around the family table.
- Focus on boosting your child's internal value through encouragement.
- Compliment and greet the person, not the body.
- Rid your home and online spaces of messages and images that promote anti-fatness.

SECTION THREE

Fear

I didn't grow up in a typical family. I had too many mothers for that.

The first was my biological mum, a feminist who stopped shaving her legs in the 1970s. Somewhat of a hippy at heart, she marched for women's rights and against apartheid, and at one point dressed our family in matching kaftans. We would wear our kaftans for family meetings held in a circle while sitting on homemade bean bags. She was the woman who birthed me and raised me, and remained my primary caregiver until I was old enough to leave home.

Next came my first stepmother: a no-nonsense, outspoken American of small stature and large presence, who arrived in our family when I was 15 and whom I loved, like family, right from the get-go. She believed strongly in social justice and encouraged my curiosity about the world with relentless and thoughtful questions.

Following her was my second stepmother, a whip-smart corporate woman who married my dad when I was 23 and remains married to him to this day. She is an exceptional role model for practising unconditional love and fiercely holding on to one's values.

And if that isn't enough mothers for one child to handle, I also had an honorary mum: a neighbour with three boys, who as far back as I can remember was my 'surrogate mother'. I met her when I was five and, almost 50 years later, a hug from her still makes the world feel kinder.

What I lacked in long-haul nuclear-family parenting, I gained in diverse voices, different opinions and the huge advantage of experiencing maternal influence from a myriad of perspectives.

One of the many flaws I possess as a mother is how easily I become one-eyed. When scared or frustrated or overwhelmed, I skitter, propelled with the accuracy and efficiency of a hungry rat towards 'solve' mode. I want things fixed. Fixed yesterday and fixed right. This overwhelming desire to fix things has become something of a warning sign for me. It signals my need for control – by which I really mean I'm frightened. The way I automatically deal with that fear is to try to get the world organised to suit me.

When I'm able to make space and notice that fear is running the show, I stop and conjure the voices of my many mothers. There is scant little the four of them would handle in exactly the same way. They have differences in opinions about food and eating, for sure. But also about bedtimes and TV, money and politics, schooling and friendships, dating, drinking, clothing – you name it. They all have (or had, in the case of my first mum) vastly different values.

Was one of them a better parent than another? No. Did one of them consistently come up with better solutions to parenting problems? No. They all did their best with the resources they had and the circumstances they faced. Each of them raised decent, imperfect humans of great depth whom I love and admire.

When the voices of these women enter my consciousness, a delightful thing happens: I lighten up. I remember there are very few absolute rights and wrongs in parenting. There is no one-size-fits-all. There are options and opportunities and ideas to try out. Their collective voices remind me that the need to be in control of others rarely ends well for anyone.

Is fear helpful to keep me from putting my hand on a hot stove? Absolutely! Is it helpful when I'm trying to make other people fall in line? Not so much. When fear is allowed to dictate our actions when we are not really in danger, no one is served well.

The very best outcomes happen when I notice my own fear and then tune my need for control away from fixing other people and instead towards how I respond to what's happening around me.

As I said, I lighten up.

When my client Bianca rang me because she couldn't get her seven-year-old son, Gabe, to sleep in his own room, she wanted to make sure she was getting the process right. She was only able to make progress after she realised how afraid she was of being a bad parent and stopped seeing Gabe's sleep routines as yet another thing she needed to master. Once she saw Gabe as capable of learning how to sleep and switched her focus from trying to make it happen to giving him the support he needed, Gabe began sleeping in his own bed almost effortlessly.

In this section, I'm going to suggest you keep your desire to fix and control in the front of your mind. In what parts of your life is fear running the show? Where can you allow your child to make mistakes in the wonderful pursuit of figuring things out for themselves? Go lightly. Be kind to yourself. Get in partnership with your child rather than dictating the terms.

In order to adopt a new perspective around health and weight, you'll need the ability to question your existing ideas and beliefs. But you're also going to need a robust tool kit equipped to deal with a much wider set of parenting challenges: effective communication, bodies and sex, eating disorders, social media and devices. And, importantly, you'll need the ability to use that tool kit with a light hand.

CHAPTER 10

Effective communication with your child

Making the brave decision to help forge cultural change is the easy bit. The far more challenging bit is going to be talking about it with your child in a way that ensures they will listen and engage. I'll give you an example.

My client Cate mentioned her frustration that her 12-year-old daughter, Lily, wouldn't listen when Cate was trying to talk to her about stereotypes and how awful our culture is to bigger people. So we looked at why Lily wasn't listening and what Cate could do to change that.

Cate originally wondered if she could set consequences for Lily's wilful ways to help her engage in certain conversations. My answer was the same as it always is: there is no appropriate consequence for not listening, and setting one will only cause further power struggles.

However, there were many things Cate could do to start having more engaging conversations with Lily. A few days after we spoke, Cate sent me this message: 'Lily is a different child. She even said, "Thanks for telling me that, Mum. I love talking to you."'

Here's what Cate and I covered.

We looked at how often Lily wouldn't listen. Was it a rare occurence or happening daily? In Lily's case, it was regular. Cate told me that it wasn't just when they were talking about bodies or food; there was an overarching sense that Lily just didn't listen much at all. Cate hated having to raise her voice louder and louder to try to get Lily's ears switched on – and it didn't seem to make any difference anyway.

If your child 'never listens', they almost certainly need you to try a different way of communicating. It could be that the lion's share of your communication is nagging and demanding (*Finish your breakfast. Pick up your jacket. Get ready. Use your deodorant.*) so they end up just blocking you out.

If your child doesn't listen, it could be that by ignoring you they are getting their power and attention needs met, as we covered earlier. Your child may know, or at least be subconsciously aware, how the system works: *All I have to do is ignore Mum and she'll be 100% focused on me.* Ignoring us certainly does the trick if they aren't getting enough power or attention elsewhere, but it's awful for us!

I encouraged Cate to see that the way she was viewing the situation wasn't helping. 'Not listening' wasn't the problem, it was a symptom: a symptom of a child feeling disengaged from their mum. Cate found our conversation challenging because she realised it was her who needed to change, not Lily. It wasn't until she understood that she could change the way she communicated with her daughter that things changed dramatically.

If you are also feeling challenged, I encourage you to take a leaf out of Cate's book and cut yourself a break. Start by reframing 'not listening' as a helpful signal that your child needs something different from you, not that they need to change. Maybe they aren't getting their power or attention needs met. Maybe they need more encouragement. Maybe they need you to be more curious and to listen without offering advice or solutions. Tweens and teens start to develop new ideas and strongly felt opinions, and having someone listen to them provides a wonderful sense of belonging and significance. I mentioned previously that kids spell love 'T.I.M.E.' They also feel loved when you listen without judgement or trying to help.

Cate decided to say thank you in her head every time Lily didn't listen. What she meant was: *Thank you for reminding me that you need me to communicate differently.* It felt empowering to Cate and she described it as if Lily had new ears.

Five ways we prevent engagement – and what to do instead

- **Too much one-way communication.** If your communication is mainly directive – *Do this, that or the other thing* – your child will switch off. Nobody likes being told what to do all the time. Try asking your child more questions and see what happens.

- **Forgetting respect.** It pays to remember that our child's activities are just as important to them as our requests are to us. Approach them with the same respect you seek in return. Instead of shouting from another room, go to where they are. Talk about what they are doing before making your request and assure them they can resume their task once they've addressed your request.
- **Spotlighting their flaws.** Rather than pointing out what they are doing wrong (*Your room is a tip! I've told you five times to clean it!*), ask a question that assumes the best (*What's your plan for cleaning your room?*). By doing this you imply they have a strategy and reinforce their internal value by demonstrating your trust in them.
- **Letting Power Time slip.** If Power Time has gone by the wayside, your child may be feeling disconnected from you and less likely to engage. Think about how you can jam it back into your routine. It's as simple as ten minutes of one-on-one time with your child on a regular basis.
- **Telling them how you feel.** Telling a child how their situation makes us feel doesn't lead to connection. They experience it as another thing to worry about. Instead of expressing our feelings (*It makes me so sad that other kids can be so mean*), validate theirs (*That sounds tough, I'm so glad you told me that*). When addressing sensitive

subjects with your child, maintaining a calm and neutral demeanour will make them more comfortable. Remaining impartial will make them more likely to listen to what you have to say.

If you follow the tips I've just described, you'll hopefully have a breakthrough in your conversations with your child. The real power, though, comes with the following tool. It's a way to broach conversations about tricky topics with our kids – and it can also bring us closer.

The Hard Conversations Scaffold

One of the tools Cate found most helpful was the Hard Conversations Scaffold. It's a game-changing structure adapted from an approach developed by parenting expert Michelle Icard. I highly recommend her book *Fourteen Talks by Age Fourteen* to all parents, particularly those who have tweens. It's a structure you can use if your child says they hate their body or they've stopped engaging in social activities because of their size. It's a flexible tool; it can also be used when talking about dieting, sex, vaping, school difficulties … There are many situations where you'll be able to use it with success.

Michelle advises us to have these 'hard' conversations *briefly and often* rather than once and done. The once-and-done approach tends to make conversations long and complex, and that doesn't work well for kids. Leave the lengthy, explore-every-avenue, in-depth discussions for a walk with a mate, and keep these chats with your kids short and simple. You want to get in and get out but you'll need to do that time and again.

If you have a teen or tween, their brain is going through huge changes. Their frontal cortex gets closed for renovations while it matures into an adult brain, so they have to use their limbic system to process emotions (and unfortunately it doesn't do a very good job). Making sure hard conversations are short but frequent will make a big difference to their ability to understand and ultimately remember the messages you're trying to convey.

The Hard Conversations Scaffold

Be calm. Begin at a place where you are both unemotional. If it helps, use a third party as a neutral entry point.

Be curious. Enter into their world as much as you can. Ask questions and repeat back what you hear.

Be human. Remind them that they are not alone in these conversations, feelings or experiences, and that they have your understanding and compassion.

Get permission, then give advice. Ask if you can share your thoughts and then it's time for the lesson or advice.

Be encouraging. Let them know you believe in them, that they are strong and capable, and that they can always ask for your help without being told off for making mistakes.

The scaffold is a structure to support your brief in-and-out conversations, rather than a particular script to use. So let's look at using it to have a conversation with our kids.

Be calm

Many of the conversations we have with our kids are governed by our desire to impart information, whether it's that they need to be wary of social-media influencers, or that their body is a good one no matter what anyone says. The lesson we want them to learn can make us anxious and feel nervous. But starting when our emotions are fired up can be a recipe for disaster.

Instead, begin when we are calm. A great way to start the conversation from a place of calm, as Michelle Icard recommends, is the side door. If you are raising an issue, you could start by mentioning a news headline or something you overheard. For example, you could say, 'A colleague said something interesting to me today. She said that girls who see weight-loss programmes advertised on social media are more likely to hate their body.' Talking about something you saw online can also be a great 'in'. Introducing a subject via a third party creates more of a calm foundation for discussion than going right to the heart of a topic.

If you're responding to an issue your child has raised, check in with your child's emotions and make sure they're calm too. If they are upset, don't talk about anything except those emotions. For example:

> 'Darling, would you like a hug?'
> 'Do you want to go and spend ten minutes in your room until you feel better?'

> 'I can imagine why you are so upset! That sounds awful. Can I make you a hot chocolate?'

Bottom line: address emotions – theirs and yours – and start from a place of calm.

Be curious

Once you've begun calmly, ask them what they think of the issue.

> 'What do you think about that statistic? Do you think that's right, or does it seem far-fetched to you?'

When Cate began starting conversations this way, she was surprised at how engaged Lily would become. Curiosity is a fabulous way of engaging in the conversation. Icard gives the brilliant advice that our kids want us to be sceptical *with* them, not *of* them. Being sceptical requires curiosity.

Curiosity requires you to ask more questions than you think might be necessary. Imagine you are writing an article and you need to know every nook and cranny of their thoughts in order to finish it. The more questions you ask, and the more you really listen to their answers, the more they will trust you and open up.

If you're talking about a topic that might have high stakes – bullying or vaping or sex, for example – remind them that you're not after names, and you're not out to blame. This is vital for tweens and teens who need to know that they won't get their friends in trouble.

They are at a developmental stage that will make them more likely to put their friendships above all else, including honesty with their parents. It's a natural and healthy part of maturity, learning how to separate themselves from us.

A great way to show them you are listening (and to make sure you really *are* listening) is to relay back to them what they've told you so you can confirm you've understood. For example, 'So, you reckon everyone kind of hates their body, so maybe it's not just girls who get weight-loss ads on social media? And kids at your school get teased about how they look?'

Be human

It can be helpful to send the message that what they are thinking or feeling is understandable, given the circumstances. And this can be a great place to share your experience (without giving advice). Bring your humanity to the conversation. For example:

> 'I'm not surprised you think that. Even in my friend group, I notice a lot of people saying they hate their bodies. Plus, I certainly hated my body when I was at intermediate school. It was a hideous feeling, and one I wish fewer people experienced.'
>
> 'If that happened to me, I'd be upset too.'
>
> 'Oh, that's an opinion shared by a lot of people, I can see how you got there.'

Get permission, then give advice

This is where you get to give them advice. It's the teaching moment you are building up to. Now that you've established trust, you get to impart your lesson. But – and this is non-negotiable, because the conversation will go pear-shaped without it – *start by asking for permission.*

> 'Can I tell you what I think?'
> 'Can I share my experience of this with you?'
> 'Would you like some ideas?'

When, and only when, they have given you permission, give your advice. Make the lesson short and move on as soon as they do. And then have the conversation again, when it's needed, and again and again. Think 15 times, rather than three.

Be encouraging

Be curious. Listen. Then encourage.

> 'You are smart, so I trust you'll figure out the best way to act for yourself.'
> 'I know you'll figure this out because I know you can do hard things.'

A mother recently emailed me to say that hearing her anxious ten-year-old say, 'I know I can do hard things,' almost made her heart burst.

* * *

If you are going to be using this scaffold over and over again, it's going to be helpful to have a trick to remember it.

Try saying this out loud: 'The calm, curious human encourages with permission.'

Write it on a sticky note and attach it to your computer. *The calm, curious human encourages with permission.* It feels good, doesn't it? Make the phrase your way to remember how to have conversations so your child will listen and engage.

That's the scaffold (and your memory trick), but I want to give you some real examples so you get to see how it works in motion. As you go through the following examples, I encourage you to build a strong foundation by practising it today, with topics that have the least emotional trigger for you. You'll start to have conversations with your child in which they fully connect and engage. The more you trust the scaffold, the more you will use it.

Using the scaffold for the 'I hate my fat [body part]' conversation

One of the most common questions I get from parents is this: 'My child says they hate their fat [body part]. What do I say?'

I hear this question from parents of children of all sizes, from the thinnest to the fattest. The conversation can be approached in pretty much the same way regardless of size, with one small difference that we will address as we go. We'll look at this conversation in two ways: how to respond when they bring the topic up themselves, and then

The calm, curious human encourages with permission.

how to bring it up with them again, remembering that, with kids, *often* trumps *once and done*. So, let's use the Hard Conversations Scaffold to tackle this example.

Imagine your child says, 'I hate my fat legs'. The most common response from parents is, 'You're not fat!'

We respond this way because we want to protect them from suffering. We mistakenly think if we tell them they are not fat they will feel better about themselves. However, if you tell them they're not fat (regardless of their actual size), instead of feeling better, two things will happen.

1. They won't believe you. They'll think you're stupid and that you don't get it, and they will be less likely to open up about their feelings again.
2. They will clam up. If you minimise their experience by telling them what they are feeling is wrong or inaccurate, they will withdraw and be left with big feelings that they can't talk to you about.

Saying 'you're not' also sends the message that being fat is really bad, and that even if you're not fat now, it's something that you shouldn't become in the future. After all, look at how badly you want to deny that they are fat.

When a child says they are 'feeling fat', they are not talking about their size. Not really. They are talking about their experience of belonging and fitting in. So addressing their size is only going to make their sense of belonging – or, in this example, not belonging – more acute.

This means if they come to you saying they feel fat, and the words *No, you're not* come into your head, best keep them to yourself and instead use the Hard Conversations Scaffold. Off we go.

Be calm

You may need to calm their emotions and possibly your own. If you need to go take a breath, let them know you've heard what they just said and that you want to talk about it but you need to pee. Shut yourself in the bathroom, breathe deeply and get yourself calm.

Then address their emotions.

> 'I'm so sorry to hear you are feeling bad. It must suck to feel like that.'

Be curious

> 'Ooof. That sounds like a horrible thing to feel. Is this the first time, or has it happened before?'
>
> 'On a scale of one to ten, how bad is this feeling? Have you talked to anyone else about it?'
>
> 'Tell me more about your legs feeling fat. Is it all the time, or just sometimes?'

Reflect back what you've heard to make sure you've got it right.

> 'So it's a five-out-of-ten bad feeling and you've been feeling that way for a while?'

Be human

'I'm really feeling for you. It's a hideous thing to feel like a part of you is wrong. It's a truly strange thing in our culture, but it's very common to not like something about our bodies. Every single person I know has something they don't like. For me, it's my nose. I'm so sorry you are having these feelings too.'

Get permission, then give advice

'Can I tell you what I think?'

'The truth is that at some point we all have to choose. We don't get to choose our body, but we do get to choose how to treat it. We can choose to focus on how it looks, or we can focus on what it does for us. Nobody gets to experience anything without their body, so it's a gift to have one, no matter what it looks like.

'Our culture is seriously mean to people who are bigger, so it's no wonder we all feel bad about our bodies. Either we are bigger and we are made to feel like our body is wrong, or we are thinner and we're taught to fear getting bigger.'

Conversation for thinner kids:

'Because your body is on the smaller side, our culture is much kinder to you than to bigger people, and in some ways it's your responsibility to help make it better for everyone. At least that's what

> we believe in our family. You are going to have to decide if you are someone who helps change our culture or allows it to stay like it is.'

Conversation for bigger-bodied kids:

> 'Because your body is on the bigger side, you might face unfair discrimination. That's tough. You do get to decide whether to stand up against that discrimination and help change our culture, but you are not expected to do that. It's a choice. You are also going to have to decide whether to treat your own body kindly, and whether to ignore the messages telling you your body isn't as good as a smaller one. It's not fair that you have to do that, but it's how it is. This will take courage.'

Be encouraging

> 'I trust you'll think about this and make the best decision for you. I believe in you. I'm here if you need support to figure out the answers for yourself.'

This can be a highly emotional topic for many parents. If that is the case for you, make sure you're as calm and detached as you can be. If you find yourself getting wound up, stop the conversation and walk away. Say something like, 'I'm so sorry, darling, can we please come back to this? I'm not feeling up to talking right now.'

Let's also go through a quick example of using the Hard Conversations Scaffold *at a later date* to bring up the topic of not liking our bodies. Let's begin at the top.

Be calm

'Hey, I saw a TikToker the other day saying she had embraced body positivity.'

Be curious

'Have you heard that term before?'

'Have you seen it used on TikTok or anywhere else?'

'Have you ever heard your friends use the term?'

'What do you think it means? Why do you think a TikToker would use it?'

Reflect on what they've told you to make sure you understand and they know you're listening:

'So you don't really know what it means, but you think you've seen it a few times? And a couple of your friends have told you they are doing it?'

Be human

'This is a topic that seems to be coming up more and more, and lots of parents are talking to their kids about it.'

Get permission, then give advice

'I have a theory. Would you like to hear it?'

Once you have been given permission, you can proceed with your advice.

'Body positivity seems to be used by a lot of people these days as a way of promoting the idea that we can love ourselves, regardless of how we look, and that we should reject messages telling us that our bodies are wrong. The idea that we can accept and be kind to our bodies instead of hate them is an idea I can really get behind. I also encourage you to do a bit of digging and find out about the origins of the body positivity movement, which is more about social change than self-love. I think both concepts are worth knowing more about, and I would love to hear about what you learn.'

Be encouraging

'There is a lot of information out there about it, so if you ever want help to find it, I'm sure you'll be able to find it easily. I'm always here if you need help.'

This way of doing things turns a hard conversation with your child into one that's about getting to know them as much as it is imparting important information. Cate told me that this felt lighter and easier than tackling the tricky stuff head-on.

Using the scaffold for a more serious/tricky conversation with older kids

The scaffold makes it easier to have conversations about serious topics like eating disorders, self-harm, drinking, vaping or sex because it gives us structure and support.

Before you begin, get yourself into a calm space, where you can bring curiosity to the surface and let go of 'protecting them' as your main concern. The older our kids get, the less we are around when they're making decisions about things like dieting or vaping or taking drugs. So communicating our trust in them is a great way to boost their confidence and encourage them to make good choices, before stepping back and letting them get on with life. Remember, this is a 'get in, get out' conversation.

Be calm

'Hey, this afternoon I read that dieting can lead to an eating disorder, and that most 14-year-olds have been on a diet by the time they get to high school.'

Be curious

'Does that sound right to you? Or does that seem overblown?'

'What do you think about dieting?'

'Do you have friends who have tried to lose weight? I don't want names, I'm just curious. Why do you think they do it?'

'Do your teachers talk about it? What do you think about their opinion?'

'If a friend asked you to diet with them, would you be tempted?'

Show them you've been listening by paraphrasing what you've heard.

'So have I got this right? You think most of your friends have dieted, and some of your mates are trying intermittent fasting at the moment, but you think it sounds really depressing? You think no one would admit to having an eating disorder, so there's no point in talking about it?'

Be human

'I know lots of parents are talking to their kids about this because it seems like so many kids are doing it. I can totally see why you say it's silly to talk about eating disorders if no one would admit to it.'

Get permission, then give advice

'Can I tell you what I've learned about dieting and eating disorders?

'To be honest, I really don't like diets because they can lead to eating disorders, which are truly awful. But, ultimately, it's your body, so you are going to have to decide for yourself if dieting is something you do or not.

> 'If you do try it, I hope you'll take the time to research it – the pros and cons – there's heaps of information online. Many doctors say it's a bad idea for young people in particular, so I just want you to know the possible consequences before you make a decision.'

Please note, if you are talking about an illegal activity here, like vaping, drugs or alcohol, let them know it's illegal at their age and ask them to consider what the consequences would be if they were to get caught.

Be encouraging

> 'I trust you to think about it before trying anything. And remember, if it feels like you've made a mistake, you can always come to me for help. I promise I'll help the best I can because I know you won't need me to say, "I told you so", or tell you off about it.'

Then change the topic.

The more you use the scaffold for all sorts of things – from finding out more about your child's interests to the more emotional, 'trickier' topics like sex, friendships or bodies – the easier it will become and the more trust you'll build with your child.

CHAPTER 11

When eating gets disordered

Having just taken you through an effective conversation with your child that links dieting with eating disorders, I would be remiss not to arm you with more information about eating disorders in general.

Back in Section One, we looked at how emotional eating is feared because it can become binge eating, and I promised that we'd look at why a beautiful thing like eating for emotional satisfaction can become disordered. The thing is, I was only giving you half the picture. We don't just fear emotional eating because it can become binge eating – and binge eating, if you have ever experienced it, can be truly horrendous. We fear it because of anti-fatness.

Now that you understand the impact that anti-fat bias has on our beliefs about food and bodies, you'll be able to see why emotional eating is so feared in our culture. It comes with the possibility of putting on weight. The fear is that if you or your child eat for emotional reasons, you'll eat more calories than if you ate only for physical or nutritional reasons, and those excess calories will make you fat.

If we can bravely put anti-fatness aside and allow our children to enjoy eating for emotional satisfaction, a strange and delightful thing can occur. Very little food will be needed to satisfy them. A couple of biscuits or a row of chocolate might do the trick. And even more surprising, once they've eaten, they will quickly move on and forget about it.

However, a different experience arises if we add anti-fatness into the equation. Fear of gaining weight makes us mentally resist the signals our body sends us to eat. If our kids try to block or ignore their appetites and desires due to what they *think* they should or shouldn't be eating, that's when things tend to go awry. They may fail to stop themselves from eating a particular food, or from eating all food. In that case, they are likely to feel guilt or shame, which then needs soothing, so they eat more to soothe the extra guilt and shame. At this point, a nasty cycle has set in that sometimes won't stop until they are in physical and emotional pain.

This cycle can also set in if someone has been resisting eating foods they really love, so they have a little bit of it because it brings such pleasure. Once they've had some, they might find themselves unable to stop, all the while telling themself they will never eat that food again, leading to eating more in case it's the last time they ever allow themselves to enjoy it. These are examples of binge eating. It's unpleasant and scary, and can lead to a very dangerous situation indeed. When binge eating becomes recurrent and uncontrollable, it constitutes a clinical eating disorder called binge-eating disorder.

Binge-eating disorders

The National Eating Disorders Association (NEDA) in the United States defines binge-eating disorder as 'a serious, life-threatening, yet treatable eating disorder characterised by recurrent episodes of eating large quantities of food, often very quickly and to the point of discomfort; a feeling of loss of control during the binge; experiencing shame, distress, or guilt afterwards, but without regularly using unhealthy compensatory measures (like purging) to counter the binge eating'.

Bulimia nervosa has all the same characteristics as binge-eating disorder with one significant difference: compensatory measures like self-induced vomiting and compulsive exercise are used to try to 'make up' for the episodes of binge eating.

Binge eating is almost always preceded by deprivation and/or restriction. A child will binge, in other words, after a period of feeling restricted. If a child has limited access to a food group (perhaps because we've placed limits on it, or because food scarcity exists), our kids may find themselves bingeing on that food (or any food) when it becomes available.

Food scarcity is one of the reasons binge eating is often present in kids in lower socio-economic situations. Binge eating is also correlated to homes where food is highly controlled, and where some foods are banned altogether.

One of the most common ways parents attempt to address binge eating is by further restriction. We remove the desired food items from their reach or stop purchasing them. When we decide to restrict what a child eats in response to a binge, we are inadvertently setting them up for more bingeing.

One of the reasons for offering kids regular opportunities to eat as much as they like – including foods high in sugar and low in nutritional value, without judgement or having what they eat linked to their body size – is that it interrupts the experience of restriction. If you suspect your child has started binge eating, I highly recommend seeking an assessment from your GP. In the meantime, I also recommend doing as much as you can to remove the experience of food restriction from your child, and to use the Hard Conversations Scaffold to talk to your child about what's going on.

When I was suffering from bulimia, I thought I was a food addict who had a broken brain when it came to food. I limited what I'd allow in the house; I tried accountability coaching; I took baths, went for walks, took personal growth seminars, did mindfulness breathing and attended group meetings – all in the name of overcoming bingeing.

If you'd told me binge eating would disappear if I simply followed the call of my body to eat what it desired and stopped being scared of fatness, I'd have thought you really didn't understand the extent of my problem. But that is what happened.

One of the most important aspects of my recovery was to stop restricting what I ate. In essence, I began to eat what my body signalled it wanted, rather than what I thought I *should* be eating. When I did that, it was remarkable how quickly and peacefully binge eating became a thing of the past.

Anorexia nervosa

NEDA characterises anorexia nervosa as a life-threatening disorder marked by self-starvation and excessive weight loss. NEDA emphasises the psychological nature of the condition, highlighting intense fears of gaining weight and distorted body image. Anorexia is not just about food; it can often be about control and deeply rooted perceptions of self-worth.

While anorexia is characterised by severe weight loss, it is also true that you don't have to be emaciated to have anorexia. Indeed, only 6% of people diagnosed with an eating disorder are classified as underweight. It is possible to have anorexia at any weight, including at the higher end of the size scale.

Corissa Enneking's story, told by Micheal Hobbs in *The Huffington Post*, is a good example of how bigger people who have anorexia can receive congratulations instead of treatment. Corissa had recently lost a large amount of weight, even though she was still too big to buy clothes from any mainstreet shops. She was starving herself, had lost her period and was having panic attacks if she broke her fast and ate. Her mother was worried about her so she took her to Emergency. When the doctor on duty was told Corissa's medical history, they advised her to 'keep up the good work' and said that her body would eventually adjust to being a thin person, at which point she could add a few hundred calories a day. No such evidence exists to back up the idea that big bodies will 'adjust' to being thin bodies. Healthcare professionals telling people who are starving themselves to 'keep it up' means that many people don't get the treatment they need or deserve. Thankfully, Corissa's mother insisted on a second opinion. Corissa was diagnosed with organ failure, due to anorexia.

If you notice your child avoiding meals, lying about what they have eaten, obsessively calorie-counting or becoming fixated on weight loss – regardless of their size – please take them to the GP to get a referral to a specialist. Remember that anorexia and other eating disorders do not have a 'look'. Understanding this will go a long way towards everyone who needs help getting it.

Orthorexia nervosa

In our quest for health and our cultural obsession with wellness, a new term has surfaced – orthorexia nervosa. NEDA describes orthorexia as an obsession with 'proper' or 'healthful' eating. But don't be deceived. On the surface, orthorexia may appear to be a dedicated pursuit of a healthy lifestyle but, underneath, it's the opposite: an unhealthy fixation on perceived dietary purity.

Individuals suffering from orthorexia will often narrow their diet to a limited array of 'safe' foods. It isn't the quantity but the 'correctness' of food that governs their choices.

Your child may start inspecting food labels meticulously or eliminating entire food groups in the name of health. But here's the thing: it's not about the food itself but the control they gain by adhering to the rules.

Orthorexia doesn't appear overnight. It comes on slowly. You might notice your child spending excessive time planning meals or displaying high levels of distress when 'healthy' foods aren't available. They may avoid social events where 'proper' food is not served.

While it may be tempting to dismiss these signs as a phase or a commitment to healthy living, remember that orthorexia, like any eating disorder, is a serious mental health disorder.

Disordered eating exists on a spectrum

It's important to understand that eating disorders and disordered eating exist on a spectrum. Disordered eating isn't a specific diagnosis like anorexia, orthorexia or binge-eating disorder. Rather, it's a range of behaviours that, while not classified as a full-blown eating disorder, can still affect a child's physical and mental health. It could be dieting that has become obsessive, or that too much time and effort is being taken up by thinking about what should and shouldn't be eaten.

What might seem like a harmless phase could swiftly become an eating disorder. The tricky part is recognising when your child's relationship with food is affecting them negatively and, if it is, how this should be tackled.

As parents, our task is to be aware of the red flags and respond quickly to catch unhealthy behaviour before it becomes toxic. Listen for diet talk or an emphasis on body size. Look out for skipped meals, overeating or a preoccupation with food that makes you uneasy. We're there to catch our kids, get them medical care if need be, offer support and love, do our best to create safe spaces for all bodies in our homes, give our children as much agency as possible, boost their internal values, and have conversations using the scaffold.

CHAPTER 12

Bodies and sex

I once had a conversation with a policeman that broke my heart. He told me that he was regularly called to break up parties where guys aged in their twenties were partying with and sometimes sleeping with teenage girls as young as 14 (and sometimes even younger).

The girls at these parties sometimes told the police, 'I never really wanted to sleep with that guy. I don't know why I didn't say no.'

I can hardly bear to think about it. *I don't know why I didn't say no.* The thought of it plays on one of the strongest instincts we collectively share as parents: to protect our children from harm. That fear might make the ideas explored in this chapter feel confronting and possibly even contradictory. How can we protect our kids while allowing them to learn from their mistakes? How can we set boundaries and make rules, while giving them enough space to learn? How do we ensure they will come to us if they need help? Where is the line between our trust and their safety?

I'm not qualified to say where exactly that line lies for you. We all have to make our own judgements about that. The amount of control I am willing to relinquish for my child, with their unique personality, experience and maturity, might be slightly or vastly different from what you are willing to let go of for yours. I won't argue about who is right or wrong. Instead, I want to raise some questions you might not have considered and look at the unintended consequences of holding on to control and not allowing our kids the freedom to make mistakes.

I want you to consider the unexpected outcomes of not letting go. My aim is to help you empower your child by consciously teaching them about sex, by giving them practice at saying no and standing up for themselves, and by fostering a respect for their body and the body autonomy of others.

The story that police officer shared illustrates what happens when poor body confidence collides with a lack of experience in speaking up for yourself. If our children do not practice standing up for how they want their bodies to be treated, and if they become used to their desires being ignored or overridden, how can they learn to speak up when they want or need to?

On the flip side, the story illustrates what can happen when a child has little practice at hearing 'no' or thinking about others. Like the young men in this story, they might grow into an adult who will believe they are entitled to have whatever they want, and act that way. Perhaps they have been modelled behaviour that told them 'no doesn't really mean no'. We'll get into that soon.

First, let's look at how we can talk about sex in general with our kids, then more specifically, what body autonomy and entitlement are and how these concepts can inform our decisions as parents. It's important to note that I'm not suggesting body autonomy is solely a female issue, and that entitlement is solely a male one. Body autonomy and entitlement affect all young people.

Body autonomy

Body autonomy is the inherent human right to have control over one's own body. This means the freedom to make decisions about one's physical self, like what to wear, what to eat and whether or not to engage in certain activities. It extends to medical decisions, personal boundaries and sexual consent. Body autonomy asserts that every person's body is their own, and nobody else can make decisions about it without their explicit consent.

When a child has body autonomy, they have the power to decide how much they eat from what is available to them, what they wear, who gets to touch them and what sexual preference they have. They know what they want and they feel able to speak up for what feels right for them.

Let's dig into clothing choices first, because parents sometimes fear their child's wardrobe choices will put them in danger. One way to handle this is to explain your reservations – let your child know you're feeling uncomfortable because of the sort of attention their outfit might attract. You can talk about how the way someone else reacts to them is that person's problem, not theirs. But you can discuss how it's also true that some choices are almost guaranteed to elicit a certain reaction, and it helps to understand that while choosing what to wear. Ultimately it's your child's decision what they wear; by giving them information and choice, you can help them make an informed decision.

There may need to be some exceptions to this rule when it comes to school dress codes, restaurant rules or places of worship. But by and large, giving your child complete agency over how they dress sends a very clear message that you respect their body autonomy.

It may go without saying, but in case you haven't considered it before, allowing your child to say no to a hug or kiss from friends and family is a great way to protect their body autonomy. Supporting them to say no to anyone who demands an unwanted kiss or cuddle indicates to them that they get to say what goes for their body. Insisting they give others the same respect is a great idea too.

Entitlement

Entitlement is when someone believes they deserve and have a right to something that is a privilege. Entitlement can manifest when we protect our children from the consequences of their actions, when they are either not able to hear or understand what someone else is saying, feeling or experiencing, or when they feel that their wants, needs and desires are more important than other people's.

Entitlement is encouraged when we prevent children from having to take responsibility for themselves in unpleasant or uncomfortable situations.

Let's look at a few examples.

When a child thinks they shouldn't have to be bored and expects a parent or teacher to solve their boredom problem for them, they feel entitled to life being fun/exciting/interesting all the time.

When a child thinks that receiving pocket money is a right not a privilege, they feel entitled to the benefits and power that come with money without having done anything to earn that power or benefit.

When a child thinks they deserve to be paid for being helpful at home, rather than knowing households predominantly run on unpaid labour, they may feel entitled to a reward for helping others and fail to understand their role in contributing to society.

When a child mistakenly believes their needs should be prioritised over and above everyone else's, they can also mistakenly think their sexual or relationship needs should too. They may think that because they have a desire to have sex, the other person does too, without necessarily checking in to make sure their assumption is accurate.

How to talk about sex with your child

Many parents imagine this is a conversation to have when their kids are older: tweens or even high-school age. However, I encourage you to start talking to your child about sex as soon as you can. When broaching this topic with your child, there are a couple of things you should keep in mind:

1. They don't come to the conversation with the same experience that you have. You come with your history plus the knowledge of everything you know is out there on the internet. That means they come with an innocence that makes the conversation very different for them than it is for you.
2. The information they need from us is vastly different from the information we needed from our parents. They have the internet. We will do well to teach them anything we don't want them googling. It is far better for them to learn what a blow job is from us, for example, than to learn what it is online.

With that in mind, here's what I suggest when it comes to conversations about sex.

For kids aged between five and ten, start with biology and how babies are made. Use the correct names for genitals. The word 'vulva', for example, should be as easy for them and us to say as the word 'arm'. I made myself say vulva over and over again when I was alone in the car until it didn't feel so hard. You can also say, 'Sex is for pleasure, but that's not going to be important until you are older and your body has changed.'

Make conversations about sex short and unemotional. Answer all their questions with as much factual information as you can.

Make these conversations about sex short and unemotional. Answer all their questions with as much factual information as you can.

For kids aged ten and over, your job is to explain everything they might hear from other kids that you don't want them learning about online. Take a moment to make a list of all the terms you can think of that they might hear from a friend, social media or a friend's older sibling. If you are not already aware, TikTok and Instagram feeds that pretend to be for young teens show sex toys and use explicit language. Even if your child doesn't have access to their own social media accounts, other children will show them these kinds of videos and images on their devices. If the idea of your child seeing a video like that and then googling terms like 'doggy style' or 'threesome' makes your blood run cold, then those are examples of terms you can explain to them.

Tips for talking about sex terms

When explaining sex terms to your child, be perfunctory. Don't make eye contact. Make sure you and your child are alone, so they don't feel embarrassed. Sit on the side of their bed so you don't have to look at them. Tell them that every kid is getting the same talk from a parent at this age because there are things they need to know about sex and it's your job as their parent to explain.

I might be making it sound like it's easy to talk about sex, but in reality, I know it's not. I had a long, giggly debrief with a mum called Sara after she had a sex conversation with her ten-year-old daughter, Kiesha. Kiesha kept her face jammed into a pillow the entire time while saying, 'Are you finished?' and squealing 'Ewww!' Sara hated every moment of it but was relieved to know her daughter wouldn't need to look online to learn the terms she'd just learned from her mother.

Teaching your child these sex terms does two things. It gives them power. If they know what someone is talking about, they won't feel silly or tempted to ask Google. Additionally, knowing about sex gives kids body confidence. If you have already talked to them about sex, they may be more likely to tell someone no, or to tell you if something has happened that they don't like.

Another thing to consider is that there may be terms on your list that you know you should explain but that you are morally against. I suggest keeping your moral position to yourself at this point. There is research to suggest that kids who are told 'not to' by parents are more likely to experiment with that very thing.

Sex can be an embarrassing topic for both parents and children to discuss. Very few of us find these conversations easy. The point is not to find a way to talk about sex with your child without embarrassment – the point is to talk about it even when you are embarrassed.

Add porn to this mix …

It's our job to teach our kids that porn isn't an accurate depiction of reality, and what to do if they see it. By all means, say to them, 'I wish

I didn't have to talk to you about this stuff, but I'm going to anyway because even if it's the last thing you want to talk to me about, I love you too much to let our awkwardness get in the way.'

The importance of talking to them about porn cannot be overstated. It's everywhere, and no matter how careful they are about avoiding it, they might end up seeing it anyway. Many kids will have seen porn by the time they are eight. So, chances are, your tween will see porn much earlier than you are prepared for.

They need to know that sex online has very little to do with sex in real life. Make a point of promising to listen and not make them feel bad if they come to you with anything they have seen or done on- or offline.

One of the messages they need to hear is that the way sex is depicted in porn gives the impression that men don't have to ask permission to have sex with women. In the vast majority of heterosexual porn (which means most of the stuff kids will see – intentionally or not), sex isn't about women at all. Consent and female pleasure are notoriously absent. The female voice is almost non-existent, making it appear like it's a young woman's job to be quiet and take it. It tells young men that sex is about their pleasure, and that women exist for their satisfaction.

It makes me want to bang heads together, starting with porn producers and distributors. But porn isn't going away, at least not in the immediate future, which makes it even more important to teach body autonomy to our kids and prevent entitlement so they're able to say no, and accept no.

When talking to your child about porn, use the Hard Conversations Scaffold to start the conversation. Jot down some side-door starters and think about the lesson you want them to learn. If you have more than one lesson, you might need to have several conversations, so that you're not tackling too much at once.

You can tell them that porn is not a representation of 'real' sex. Most people's genitals look nothing like what you see in porn (you can remind them about how easy it is for videos to be edited, and tell them that's what happens in the porn industry). Most heterosexual porn is about male pleasure, even though real sex should be about the pleasure of both genders.

For conversations about sex and porn, you can also use the 'drop and run' method of teaching. Tell them there are things they have to learn and you recognise they probably don't want to hear them from you. Then send them to websites you know are safe and leave them to learn for themselves. You'll find resources on page 281.

Have you taught your child to respect your 'no'?

Let's look at the use of the word 'no' in your household. Does no really mean no, or is it more of a 'sometimes', 'maybe', or 'oh, go on then'? Is it an invitation to argue, ignore or negotiate until a 'no' becomes a 'yes'? Do your kids know that if they whinge, push, plead and persuade, you'll be worn down to a 'yes'? Or perhaps a 'no' is something they can get the other parent to override?

You may be thinking, *But hang on, sometimes they do come up with a good argument. Sometimes they do persuade me.* One way to think about this is to think about how it feels when you give in. Is it because it's just too hard to deal with the badgering? Do they know that if they squeeze hard enough, you'll back down?

Or do they know that if you say no, you mean it?

If it's more of the former and less of the latter, now is the time to start having a different relationship with the word 'no'. Tell your children that you've trained them into thinking your no doesn't really mean no. Tell them that from now on, if you say no, you're going to stick to your word and that you'll also let them know if/when you're open to being persuaded.

That conversation might look like this: 'No, you can't go to the movies tonight. The reason I'm saying no is that you haven't done your chores and you are supposed to be talking with your grandma on the phone later. If you can convince me that those things will get done, I'm open to changing my mind.'

You could try being more considered with your 'no's. You could say, 'I'm not sure yet; let me have some time to think about it.'

In my house, if kids ask again when I've already said no, I use Amy McCready's suggestion to respond along the lines of, 'You've already asked me that and I've given my answer. You are not going to get a different answer to the same question simply by asking it again.'

Do you respect their 'no'?

Let's look at how we can respect our kids when they say no. This is great practice for them when they need to say no in more serious situations. You may already be baulking at this. If we respected every no we received from our children, would they ever contribute to household chores or learn to do the hard stuff that takes courage and perseverance?

Can you please empty the dishwasher? *No.*

Can you please stop pulling your brother's hair? *No.*

Can you please stop that game now and get in the car? *No.*

I'm not suggesting you respect every single no they ever say, but I am suggesting you consider how to respect a lot more than you currently do, and pay particular attention to the times they are defending their bodily autonomy. For example, when your child says no to having their hair cut, or if they don't want to add another layer of clothing because they say they feel warm enough, or when they don't want to stop running when you've asked them to walk.

The point here is to notice the relationship you and your children have with the word no and start tweaking it to make it more powerful.

Puberty

There are plenty of great books, podcasts and online information that can help you support your child through puberty. I encourage you to learn about the physical and emotional changes that transform their identities, bodies, brains and self-esteem, and their relationships with their parents and peers. In the process, keep in mind that the internal changes we can't see are just as significant as the external ones so brutally obvious to the world.

I'm not going to go into all the changes your child might experience. I am going to suggest how you can tell the difference between the typical, to-be-expected body anxieties your child may feel as their body changes, and the more serious red flags.

As children grapple with changes in their physique, they may feel self-conscious, unsure or even alienated from their own bodies. This is normal. During puberty, they are biologically driven to move away from us and towards their peers. One way this manifests is a desire to make themselves look more similar to their peer group than to us. That's why groups of teens often all style their hair the same way, and it's also why trends and fads have such a strong influence on young people. The challenging part of this is that they may question their sense of belonging if, in their mind, they look 'wrong'. They are not being silly; in their mind it really is true. This is why, during puberty, comments about hating how they look are more common. It's even more critical at this stage to listen to and humanise their experience. Your Hard Conversations Scaffold is going to be particularly useful during this time.

It's equally important not to try to fix their pain for them or to burden them with your emotions about what they are experiencing. Their sense of not wanting to hurt you can be very strong at this stage of their lives, even though they might seem to have no empathy at all.

Typical body insecurity can become sinister when it has a significant impact on your child's ability to socialise. It's normal for them to occasionally criticise the way they look or stress about what to wear. They may even once or twice decide they can't go somewhere because they don't have the right outfit. However, when they can't go out repeatedly due to how they look, a more serious issue may have set in.

They may stress about their bathing suit and need to find one that covers them up more than they used to, but if they refuse to swim altogether, that can be a red flag.

They may miss the odd meal because they've just had a snack and are no longer hungry, or they just don't need that much that day. But if refusing to eat becomes an ongoing issue and is accompanied by negative body comments, this could signal something more serious.

The bottom line is that if you have concerns, it's best to talk to your doctor or your healthcare provider without your child (it's perfectly fine to make an appointment to talk about them - in fact, I recommend it) and get a plan in place to help them if need be. I suggest being extra vigilant at this point about making your home a place devoid of anti-fatness.

CHAPTER 13

Sleep

My husband has the insufferable ability to sleep anywhere: in a car, a plane, a ship or movie theatre; it doesn't matter. He doesn't have to be lying down or in a darkened room. All he has to do is close his eyes and he sleeps. I wasn't fitted with such luck. It takes a hard-core sleeping pill to put me out on a long-haul flight. If I so much as think about wine, I toss and turn all night. And then in my late forties, like many women, I got insomnia. It snuck up on me in a stealth suit and settled in so quietly I had no awareness of the impact on me or my family – not until a therapist told me how dire my situation was.

Of course, I knew I had trouble sleeping. I knew I was tired. I knew I was grumpy because I was tired. But I had convinced myself that I was handling it. I'd read every book on the subject that I could find and every so often I slept through the night. I just thought, at my age, women had to deal with a touch of sleep deprivation.

Then, during a very uncomfortable exchange with my therapist, I learned that if I didn't take responsibility for sleeping, she couldn't work with me. And as if that wasn't hard enough to hear, she added, 'If you can't sleep, you can't expect your relationship to work.' I hated her a little bit right then. I mean, I'd turned up to therapy to fix my husband. In no uncertain terms, I was being told that a large part of our problem was me. Now that I do sleep and my bruised ego has recovered, I count that exchange as one of the most helpful in my life. I've come to feel nothing but gratitude and respect for that therapist.

Wanting my relationship to work and not wanting to live on the edge of sleep deprivation was motivation enough for me to engage a sleep coach. Long story short, I now sleep.

All of which is why I'm so excited for you to get sleep transformed in your family if it isn't currently as good as it could be.

It's common knowledge that sleep is fundamental to overall wellbeing, but you may not be so familiar with sleep's role in developing good body confidence. It's hard for kids to try new foods or tune into their hunger and fullness cues if they are sleep deprived, yet both things are necessary for them to become competent eaters. Sleep is also necessary for children to learn to feel connected to their bodies and able to handle their emotions.

Many researchers warn that teen sleep deprivation is a serious problem. Indeed, symptoms of sleep deprivation can be similar to those of ADHD and other neurological and behavioural conditions. Sleep deprivation can affect hunger, self-esteem, performance at school and in sport, driving, motivation and emotional regulation. In other words, helping your child sleep well can pay big dividends in both body confidence and general wellbeing.

If you suspect your child is sleep deprived, you can start to help them by assessing what kind of sleep problem they might have.

Assessing sleep in your family

If sleep is causing you stress, anxiety or dread, or provoking arguments between you and your partner, or if your child is waking up tired, the first question to answer is whether you need to seek a medical opinion.

Does your child snore regularly and loudly when they are asleep, mouth breathe, or dribble profusely (but isn't teething)?

A healthy child will not regularly snore or make excessive noise while sleeping. If your child does, they should be assessed for sleep apnoea by a trained medical professional. No amount of sleep training, Power Time, routine building or encouragement will help your child sleep better if they have sleep apnoea, so if this might be the case, book an appointment with your GP.

On the other hand, if your child is typically a quiet sleeper but struggles to fall asleep, comes into your room at night, wakes up unrested or cranky, or sleeps an extra hour or two on the weekends (tweens and teens may do this, but it can be a sign of sleep deprivation if it's frequently happening pre-puberty), then I suggest assessing your child's sleep routine and making some adjustments.

What's the goal?

Let's begin by casting back to Section One. Remember how we shifted from the goal of *making our kids eat* to *helping our kids become competent eaters*? I suggest approaching sleep the same way. We can no more *make* our child sleep well than *make* them eat well.

Going to sleep is another of those things a child has 100% control over. Therefore, instead of seeing our job as making our child sleep well on a daily basis (which we can't actually do), our job is to create an environment where our child can become a *competent sleeper.*

Sleeping competence

A competent sleeper of any age is one who gets enough sleep for their unique needs. They will:

- fall asleep within 15 to 20 minutes of lights out,
- fall asleep without outside assistance,
- sleep through the night most nights,
- normally wake up refreshed,
- nap appropriately for their age,
- and function well during the day.

Your child is probably not getting enough sleep if any of the following things are happening:

- Bedtime includes power struggles, fights and frustrating behaviour.
- They fall asleep the instant their head hits the pillow.
- They need you to be with them to get to sleep.
- They take a while to wake up and are cranky in the morning, or they need to sleep an extra few hours on the weekends.

Seven non-medical reasons for sleep problems

1. **Lack of routine.** They don't know what will happen tonight because bedtime is a bit different each day. Without a routine, they will negotiate, which can make it hard for them to fall asleep easily. Without a routine, forming a sleep habit can be challenging.
2. **Lack of consistency with the routine.** They don't know if the routine will be enforced tonight, so they'll try to make changes. Having day-in-day-out consistency that doesn't change over the weekend will help your child's sleep become habitual.
3. **They use bedtime to get their attention and power needs met.** They get their daily needs met at bedtime because they haven't had enough time or attention from you during the day.
4. **Watching screens too close to bedtime.** The light from using a device suppresses their melatonin production.

Melatonin is a hormone needed to fall asleep. Humans of all ages need at least an hour of screen-free time for melatonin to build up sufficiently to fall asleep.

5. **Can't fall asleep without outside help.** They need you to rub their back or lie in their bed. A competent sleeper can get themselves to sleep without you or a crutch to rely on.
6. **Using rewards to motivate.** Paying a teen to follow a routine might work in the short term. However, short-term is the name of the rewards game, and we're playing a long game here.
7. **Bedtime is too early.** Getting kids to bed when they are not tired doesn't work and they will act up. Natural tiredness for tweens and teens may kick in much later than it did when they were younger.

Getting started

You can start by making a note of areas where your child is already competent and where they need support. The fundamental premise of teaching your child sleeping competence is to put them in charge as much as possible.

Take a few moments now to jot down ways to give your child more control during their sleep routine and during their life in general. Make a plan to implement those ideas and involve your child in the process. Remind them they are growing up and developing maturity, so it's time for them to do more for themselves, and let them know that you want them to take charge of getting themselves into a good sleep routine. You can do this with kids as young as five, and it's imperative you do it with kids over the age of eight.

In addition to your own ideas about adding more agency to their sleep routine, I recommend looking online for guidance on creating age-appropriate sleep routines. There are links to some great resources on my website (you can find a link on page 280) – they could be a good place to start.

Here are two things to remember along the way:

1. Helping your child to develop sleeping competence will require upfront time and energy. When I make sleep competence suggestions to some parents, they baulk because they can't see any extra time in their day. I, too, am a busy parent so I understand how overwhelming the idea of a time-consuming parenting suggestion can feel. Put a timeframe around trying new strategies. Give things a considered effort for two weeks and see if it's worth it.
2. When the going gets tough, remember that sleep competence goes beyond health and body confidence. Children with clear boundaries and routines (during the day or night) feel safer than those without. A child's sense of safety can affect their internal value.

At this point, you may be wondering, *What if I'm one of those parents who just can't handle it?* Or maybe, *Do I have one of those kids who just won't respond to a sleep routine?* Or, *We've tried to make changes, but it's just not working – or only seems to be making things worse.* Please be very kind to yourself. Sleep training can be extremely hard, and the basics simply don't work with some kids. If you try for a month and it's only causing you more stress, please stop. It doesn't mean there is something wrong with you or your child. It's that the training doesn't work for you. If it's within your means, you could try hiring a sleep consultant for more specific help, or you can let it go and focus on other areas to build your child's confidence.

CHAPTER 14

Social media and device competence

Every parent I know has a different approach to social media and devices. Perhaps you're a no-holds-barred family where your child gets unfettered access, or maybe you're a ban-all-access-completely family. Most of us sit somewhere between those two extremes. What we all have in common is being among the first generation of parents who have kids with access to the internet, smartphones and social media. Being first is tough – we're flying blind.

Whether it's the fear of what they have access to, the potential danger to their mental health or body image, or the fear that our children will lose the ability to partake in face-to-face communication, screens add to the load of modern parenting.

What's the goal?

So where to start? What's our goal when it comes to kids using social media and devices? It's the same approach as for food and sleep. Do we want our kids to simply obey our rules because we know better than them (and believe me, I understand the temptation there!) or do we want our kids to be competent social-media users who can self-regulate and be discerning? Once again, the problem with us taking the position of ultimate authority is that it doesn't allow our kids to learn good habits through experience.

Even if we did want to ban them from social media and prevent them from seeing adult content, I don't know if there is actually a way to completely prevent a child from accessing the internet and everything available on it. You'd have to ban visits to other people's houses, avoid social situations with other children, and homeschool your kids. But perhaps the worst thing we can do is set up a situation where our kids sneak away and hide what they are doing online. Doing that means they will then feel unable to come to us if something has disturbed them. If our kids are too frightened of being told off if they confess to seeing something they are banned from, we lose the ability to help them deal with what's happened.

The alternative is to teach them device competence. This is about helping a child to use technology with respect, discernment and self-regulation.

Take a moment to think about what it will be like in your house to have a child who manages their own device use. They put controllers, remotes, laptops or iPads away the first time you ask. They take all devices out of their rooms at the agreed time in the evening without prompting. They tell you if they have seen something that makes them feel bad or uncomfortable. And if they see something online that makes them feel bad about how they look, they know that something is wrong with what they are looking at, not with them. That is device competence at work.

If a child has device competence, they:

- use devices the same way whether you are in the room or not,
- are free to tell you about what they're seeing or watching,
- know the dangers and the positives of the internet,
- and understand and respect the rules of the household.

When it comes to body image, our kids' access to the internet can affect them in two different ways: it can harm body confidence or promote it. They can be exposed to unhelpful messages, be bullied by peers, receive mean comments about how they look or what they eat, and see misinformation about food and bodies. On the positive side, the internet can expose them to body diversity, body positivity and a range of helpful food and weight information. It can help them learn more about practising body autonomy and allow them to connect with people who are changing our culture in favourable ways when it comes to food and weight.

Before we get into the nitty-gritty, you might want to pause and take a deep breath. If your child has had few screen boundaries in the past, the ideas you're about to learn in this chapter might be difficult for you to implement, and they might be challenging to your child because, most likely, they won't be too happy about the changes. On the other hand, if you've been ruling with an iron fist, it might be you who feels more challenged while your child enjoys the changes! I encourage you to read through the suggestions and see them as just that: suggestions, not hard-and-fast rules. Parenting kids in the digital age means we're navigating a new frontier, so go easy on yourself – and your kids.

Start with the positives

In conversations with friends and parenting groups, I've noticed that devices are almost always talked about in negative terms. The addictiveness. The threat to kids' body image. The bullying. The dangers of being groomed. The access to porn. The impact on mental health. The behaviour of kids after they've had a lot of access (you know that one, right?).

What's often missed in these conversations is a discussion of the positive side of devices. Access to creative tools like photography, video and graphic design. Communication and sharing tools. Learning and research. Music. Ideas. The devices our children have are powerful instruments that can be used to educate, create, connect and entertain. From a young age, our kids see all that goodness and want to know that we do too.

That's why I recommend you start by thinking about the benefits your child enjoys when it comes to these devices. Consider everything from the TV through to their smartphone, and focus on all the benefits they get from them. If they don't have their own phone yet, imagine the pleasure and enjoyment they could potentially get from having one. If they do have one, focus for a moment on the positives.

When we are busy opposing the use of their devices and fighting with our kids about them, we lose the opportunity to connect with them about something that plays a crucial role in their lives. The trick is to help them learn to use devices so the benefits are amplified and the drawbacks are minimised.

At the same time as looking at the positives, we should not minimise or disregard the potential dangers. So how do we navigate this? How do we acknowledge the awesomeness of devices, while being mindful of the downside?

No good tool comes without dangers

Michelle Icard suggests approaching devices with the same caution as you would any other dangerous tool (the more dangerous the tool, in fact, the more useful it tends to be), and I think that is great advice. Icard makes the point that we wouldn't consider giving our child a sharp knife without teaching them how to use it correctly; we would give them training to help them become competent at using sharp tools without hurting themselves. The same goes for teaching our kids to use technology.

Teaching them device competence means shifting our thinking away from monitoring and controlling and towards training them

Whether your child is a toddler or a teen, the most important concept is that access to devices is a privilege not a right, and with privilege comes responsibility. As kids mature, their access to technology and apps can expand, and so will their responsibility to use them appropriately.

appropriately. You'll be calling on many of the tools you've already learned, like supporting rather than managing, setting appropriate consequences, giving agency and attention, and using the Hard Conversations Scaffold – all the while ensuring that their sense of internal value, rather than their external value, is being promoted.

Whether your child is a toddler or a teen, the most important concept is that access to devices is a privilege not a right, and with privilege comes responsibility. As kids mature, their access to technology and apps can expand, and so will their responsibility to use them appropriately.

Before we look at the main tool for teaching them device competence, let's look at a few traps we as parents can fall into and how to get out of them.

Common traps

Trap #1: The rules are too complicated

To learn to be competent device users, straightforward rules are essential because they are easier to follow. Make sure your child completely understands the rules and the consequences of not following them. I suggest they can recite them by heart.

Trap #2: Your children are over-entertained

Believe me, I get how devices can make life easier when dealing with bored kids. Nothing is quite as effective as a device if you need instant peace and quiet. And sometimes we do need it. The question is: do we believe our child has the chops to figure out how to entertain themselves without a device? Creativity is often fuelled by boredom. When a child is expected time and again to deal with boredom without the help of a device, we show our confidence that they can solve that boredom for themselves.

Trap #3: You're not following your own rules

Teenagers can sniff out hypocrisy from a hundred paces. If you don't follow the rules you give your child, you need to have very clear, understandable reasons why not. Otherwise, follow the rules yourself.

Trap #4: You don't know what your kids are doing

Do you know what they are doing on their devices or online? Do you know the kind of language they are using to make comments? Do you know if they have notifications turned on or off? Do you know what is cool with their friends and what isn't? Learning more about their digital world will open up a line of communication that could help make them safer.

Trap #5: You don't have any device-free time or spaces

Do you have a couple of times or places for your family that are device-free? Consider making mealtimes or Sundays or car-rides no-device zones. That means *everyone* puts their phone on silent or out of the room or only uses them for communal music – and, yes, this includes you, even if you're expecting an important work call or text. If you haven't considered having a no-device policy in the car, let me tell you about the benefits. Driving is one of the best times for talking, particularly with tweens/teens. Also, if we take a quick glance at a text while driving, our kids will think that it's fine to do that when they start driving.

* * *

At this point, you might be thinking, *But I'm too far gone. They haven't had training or rules; it will be a nightmare if I instigate no-devices policies when they've become so used to constant access.*

If you want your child to have increased device competence, it's important you don't simply change the rules without making sure they know what's coming well in advance. Setting up a Healthy Online Engagement Contract is a great way to indicate that changes are coming, even if your child has had no concrete device responsibilities up until now.

The Healthy Online Engagement Contract

The Healthy Online Engagement Contract is one of my favourite parenting tools. It improves children's discernment and puts the responsibility for using one of their favourite things into their hands.

The contract is loosely based on a tech contract designed by Amy McCready from Positive Parenting Solutions and adjusted to support a healthy relationship with food and the body.

The very first step is to let your child know a device contract is coming, and tell them why. Use the Hard Conversations Scaffold to get a feel for where they are at with their devices and what they think constitutes healthy engagement. You might start by saying, 'I heard an interesting statistic about kids and devices today…' Then you could talk about how experts are suggesting clear rules and training, and then ask, 'What do you think about our rules? Do you think we could do better?'

If you get permission to give them your opinion, say something along the lines of: 'I believe that using devices and social media isn't a right, it's a privilege. And with that privilege comes some responsibilities. I believe you're old enough now to be in charge of your devices instead of being policed by me. For that we need an official agreement about what your responsibilities are. How about we both think about what should be in it, and then write it together? I'm genuinely curious to know your thoughts on this.'

Having this conversation with a preschooler is obviously different from having it with older kids. You can, however, adjust the conversation to any level. Even preschoolers can understand that not everyone gets to watch TV (it's a privilege) and that there are things they have to do (their responsibility) in order to enjoy that privilege. Tell them they are growing up and they need to be able to manage it themselves rather than be told what to do like a baby.

The key elements are to define:

- what is the privilege (for example, using the iPad),
- what is their responsibility (using a timer and returning the iPad to its place),
- and what is the consequence of forgetting their responsibility (no iPad for a week).

Remember, if they haven't had rules previously, they are likely to push back hard when the idea of a contract is being mooted and when the rules are implemented. It may take a few weeks, or even months, for them to understand that you are serious about their responsibilities and the consequences of their choices.

If there has been constant tension between you about devices in your house, you can use this as a way to initiate a conversation about implementing a contract. Say that you hate how much you're fighting and you imagine they don't like it either. Tell them the goal is for them to be able to use devices in the house responsibly without having anyone police them.

If they get upset when it's time to sign the contract, make it clear that they don't have to. They can choose to not have access to social media or a device. If they choose not to, tell them you'll put their devices away for a couple of months until they have developed the maturity to handle the responsibility. Remember that no means no, so if they haven't calmed down, show them on the calendar when you'll revisit the conversation again. Resist the urge to revisit earlier than you said (I can just about guarantee they will try to get you to). This will boost their respect for the contract, reinforce that no means no and improve their motivation to use their device responsibly.

How to create your Healthy Online Engagement Contract

When your child is ready and willing to take on the responsibility that goes with using devices, you'll find a link on page 281 in the resources section where you can download an editable contract. Or you can create your own.

At the top of the contract, state their name and that they agree to the following social-media and device rules.

Create a checkbox of the training topics they need to have covered to get full device privileges. Here are some examples of areas to cover.

What to do if your younger child sees something upsetting (including porn)

Let your child know that if they see something upsetting then it was probably meant for adults and that they should move away from the device and come and tell you or another adult. Explain that there is a lot of stuff on the internet that isn't meant for them so they need to be prepared to talk about it if they see it.

Include a conversation about what to do if they see porn. Use the websites listed on page 281 of the resources section to help you have an age-appropriate conversation.

Get your child to practise what to do if they see something that upsets them, so they know exactly what to do when it happens.

Porn conversation for tweens and older

As kids get older, watching porn may no longer feel upsetting. It could be exciting, fun, scary or enticing. Those feelings may be confusing and make a child feel ashamed or dirty. Normalising how porn can make people feel and having healthy conversations about the prevalence of porn will help your child stay as safe as possible.

Aim to be someone your child can talk to and ensure that they know where to get safe, helpful information. On page 281 of the resources section, I list some websites that will help you; they have conversation starters that you can use.

Open videos for your child to watch on safe, helpful sites and then leave them to watch the videos on their own; let them know you are there to answer any questions if they have them.

Online bullying

Begin by asking your child: 'What do you think online bullying means?' Get as much information from them as you can.

If they don't know what it is, explain it to them. Online bullying is when kids intimidate, harass or threaten others online through apps, texts or email. It can include sharing harmful, false or malicious words or pictures about another child, leading to them feeling upset and distressed. It can feel so awful they don't feel safe going to school. Online bullying can start innocently, when a comment is made that has no intent to harm but which can be taken the wrong way and shared by others. Online bullying isn't simply saying something mean once; it's when it's ongoing and has the intention of scaring or harming someone over a period of time.

Explain why it's so serious in an unemotional, straightforward way. For example, 'Online bullying can be really upsetting for kids. It is one of the leading factors when it comes to teen suicide, so it's really important that we take it seriously.' Explain that making fun of someone's body is the most common form of online bullying, and it's also the type of bullying that a school is least likely to do anything about. Use the Hard Conversations Scaffold to discuss why that is and what your child thinks is their responsibility.

If your child is larger, you can make it clear that social norms and the bully are at fault, not them. If they are thin, let them know their body size comes with social benefits that are not earned and which make it seem as if thinness is morally superior to fatness. It is the responsibility of thin people to advocate for social change and tackle bullying when they see it.

Get them to role-play different scenarios with you. Pretend they have seen bullying happening; get them to say what they should do and who they should tell. Also role-play what happens if they have been accused of bullying themselves.

By role-play I mean that first you pretend to be the child who has seen something they need to tell an adult about and they pretend to be the adult. Then switch roles.

Just because you have talked to them about bullying – and role-played different scenarios – doesn't guarantee they won't bully others or know what to do if they are bullied. But it will make them more prepared than if you don't. It will also make them think about what they do or see in ways they may not if you didn't take time to train them. It can be extremely hard to stand up to friends and go against a crowd that is bullying someone (particularly for tweens and teens), or to get help if they are on the receiving end, so returning to this training more than once is a good idea.

Sharing personal information about others

Ask them what they know about this. One of the promises you can make to your children is not to share any images of them anywhere online without their express permission. It may surprise you how strong your child's opinion about this is.

If they already have social media, go through some of the photos they've posted and ask them how they got permission to use the images. Role-play asking for permission if necessary.

If you have followed my social-media accounts, you may have noticed that I almost never share pictures of my children. That's because they've told me they don't want me to, and I respect that. Asking for permission to share is a fantastic way to teach them about consent, respect and boundaries.

Image and video manipulation

Until the advent of the smartphone, photo editing was largely limited to billboards and magazines. These days, everyone has powerful photo- and video-editing software in their pocket.

Talk to your kids about this. Look at images together and ask if they can tell whether they have been digitally altered or not. Discuss how sometimes it's easy to tell but, more often than not, it's impossible. Ask if the images you're looking at are a reflection of reality. Discuss why people feel the need to change how they look. Doing this will help them understand that what they see in the mirror won't necessarily look like what they see on screens, because the mirror doesn't have filters or Photoshop. It will also help them to think about what they are doing rather than just use filters mindlessly.

The good thing is that kids as young as five can understand that images can be altered. Find a clip that shows a video being edited in real time and watch it with your child. Find ones that show how people can be edited while singing or dancing.

Choose a video that changes skin and hair colour, shifts body size and applies makeup digitally. Ask if they can tell the difference between what the kids in their class look like and what the kids in videos look like. Are they the same? How are they different? Why do they think that is?

After doing this training, you might see an immediate shift in your child. You may notice them say things like, 'I wonder how long that girl's neck really is?' when they are watching a show they like.

If a child makes comments like that, it means they understand that media isn't always a reflection of reality. There is space between what they watch and their understanding of what the real world looks like.

I recommend coming back to this training regularly to remind your children of the differences between online imagery and the real world. You can drive this point home as much as you like.

Spotting stereotypes

Start by asking your kids what they think a stereotype is. Ask them to make a list of all the stereotypes they can think of. What is the stereotype of a runner? A CEO? A librarian? Get as wacky as you like.

Then talk about how stereotypes harm people if they start to think that the stereotype is a given. You *have* to be slim to be a runner or a yogi. You *have* to be a man to be CEO. You *have* to have grey hair and glasses to be a librarian.

Spend time on TikTok or Instagram or YouTube with the express purpose of spotting stereotypes with your child.

Ask them to start calling out stereotypes when they see them from now on. Ask them how it would feel for people to jump to conclusions about them based on the way they look.

Ensuring diversity

When you've done the stereotype training it's time for diversity training. This is where you can raise the idea that seeing a diverse range of people doing different things is healthy. Analyse different social accounts for diversity of all kinds. Make diversity in your child's social feeds a prerequisite for the privilege of using social media. Insisting on this one requirement for social media will go a long way to helping your child feel like their body is just another body in the vast variety of bodies that exist. That's a good thing when it comes to body confidence.

Curating content for empowerment

Set them up to understand that, ultimately, they get to decide how they feel about themselves when using their devices. Let them know that if someone, anyone, anything, makes them feel like their body isn't right – that it's the wrong shape or height or weight or colour, or whatever – then there is something wrong with that message, not with their body. Ask your child to check in with themselves from time to time by asking themselves, *How does this information make me feel? Does it make me feel like I need to change my body or that my body is not worth taking care of?* Remind them that they are free to block, report or delete any content that makes them feel bad about themselves.

Let them know that if you see they are following an account that would make you feel bad about yourself, you're going to let them know, and let them know why. Tell them you're not going to make them block it or delete it, but you are going to talk about it and they need to be open to those conversations.

The reason it isn't a good idea to insist on blocking or deleting anything is that allowing them to make the choice acknowledges their agency. If they are free to do what they want, they are more likely to challenge what they are looking at than simply feel policed and defiant.

The ABCs of responsible scrolling

Training your child how to deal with information they find online in an empowering, pragmatic way is an important aspect of learning healthy online engagement. The ABCs of responsible scrolling is a simple tool that even young primary-school kids can learn.

> **A is for Arrest (or stop).** Remember not everything you read online is true. Take a moment to notice how what you're reading

or looking at makes you feel. Are you engaged because you want what they are selling, because you're intrigued by the information, or something else?

B is for Breathe. Take a couple of deep breaths.

C is for Check. Where does this information come from? Has it been fact checked? What is the purpose of the post?

Spend some time watching media and get your child to practise using the ABCs to show you they can use social media responsibly.

After listing the training your child needs to do, you can specify the other things they'll need to agree to for the privilege of using devices. A tween, for example, might also agree to have all devices out of their room by 8.00 pm. Think about the device management you want your child to take care of without being reminded by you (shut down, plug in, remove from room and put in designated area), and make those things their job. A younger child will have different rules and a different list from an older one. Theirs might include putting on a timer for the allocated time and returning a device or controller to where it lives afterwards.

Below the training and responsibilities requirements is the final section of the contract. This section states the consequences of not following the responsibilities that come with the privilege of having a device and access to social media. I suggest co-creating the consequences with your child, as it gives them agency and long-term buy-in. Lastly, you both sign and date the contract.

This is a good moment to remember that the goal of the Healthy Online Engagement Contract is not *just* about keeping your child safe. It's about teaching them competence. That means the goal isn't to ensure they always use devices perfectly or that they never have a bad experience. Even with this contract and the training they get, they are likely to see unhelpful messages and probably follow unhelpful accounts. The goal is to set the scene for them to think about how they use their devices, to be critical of what they are looking at, and to put some space between what they see and their view of themselves.

Ultimately, a child who has good critical-thinking habits and a good level of internal value is far more likely to enjoy body confidence than a child who doesn't. For that reason, I suggest making the contract valid for one year so you can revisit the training on an annual basis.

When you create the contract, be mindful of making it work for you and your family. Consider all the ideas here as suggestions rather than what you 'should' be doing. The more you are able to negotiate parts of the contract with your child, the more buy-in you will get and the smoother things will go.

Summary of Section Three

- To have conversations where children will listen, we need to engage with them, earn their trust and do more listening than talking.
- When our kids say things about their bodies, we need to listen and support them rather than trying to fix and solve their issues.
- Sleep can have a big impact on body confidence, and we can train for long-term competence.
- Eating disorders come in many forms, and it pays to understand the red flags and know what to look out for.
- It's our job to teach our kids about sex and porn so they don't ask Google for information and risk being exposed to potentially upsetting images.
- It is typical to experience more body consciousness during puberty. It's when body consciousness starts to get in the way of socialising on a regular basis that a problem might arise.
- We can train our kids to use devices well from a young age. Teaching them competence will have better long-term results than strict rules.

Parenting tips

- Use the Hard Conversations Scaffold for tricky conversations – remember: the calm, curious human encourages with permission.

- Help your child create a sleep routine that they are in charge of.
- Use a Healthy Online Engagement Screen Contract to help your child become a competent device user.
- Provide a device training plan for your child that includes adding diversity, spotting stereotypes, what to do if they see upsetting content and how to check if info is valid.

Final words

Have you ever assembled flat-pack furniture? While it might not be the easiest task, it does usually come replete with step-by-step guidance. It doesn't matter who follows the guide: a piece of furniture will emerge intact if the instructions are followed.

As we know, such a thing does not exist for children. More to the point, that manual we might wish for would look entirely different from one child to the next. That's true not only because each child is different, but because each parent is too. While I can't give you any form of bespoke child manual, what I can tell you is that spending time trying to figure out the perfect place to start is not as helpful as simply making a start. It doesn't matter where you begin; all that matters is that you do.

The one thing I caution against, though, is trying to do everything at once. Maybe you're eager to teach them eating competence, sort out their bedtime routine and instigate a screen contract. I encourage you to pause for a moment and give yourself time to make changes in stages. It's probably going to be a much smoother process if you introduce these ideas one after the other, rather than trying to get it all sorted this month.

Begin by thinking about two or three things you can change about yourself. Here are some questions I encourage you to ask:

- How can I listen more and make fewer demands?
- Where can I let go and be more relaxed?
- How can I be more supportive and less directive?
- Where can I let them take more control?

Give yourself permission to focus on one of these for a week at a time. See what happens. Notice how different you are when you do these things and notice the reaction of your child.

After you've started to see some shifts, go back through this book again and write down more changes you want to make. Maybe it's decluttering your home of negative messages or changing your health and wellness goals. Again, pace yourself and be mindful of not trying to do too much at once.

Your food competence and body confidence

I've come a long way since holding my babies in my arms and promising: *I'm not going to let you feel the same way about your body and the way you eat as I did.* Here's what I've come to know.

If you're alive, you have a body that requires nourishment. Everyone on the planet is descended from hundreds of thousands of years of bodies that ate food. Some guardians of diet culture will try to convince us that there is only one correct way to look and eat, but they are mistaken – and also annoying.

We all have a body, and part of the design is that we are fitted with the most remarkable mechanisms to eat what is right for us. Even if you've dieted constantly from a young age, your body's signals still lurk within. Your hunger and fullness and emotional-satisfaction cues are patiently waiting for you to pay attention.

Your body and your appetite are perfectly conceived to tell you what you need. Even if you've stopped listening, they've not gone anywhere. You do not need authorisation from me or anybody else to trust your body and have a healthy relationship with food. But in case no one has ever told you before, you are 100% allowed to eat what you want and treat your body with the respect it's worthy of.

It's one thing hearing that from me, but how can you trust yourself? How can you accept your body and have a healthy relationship with food, if this has been so far from your experience in the past?

Worthiness

In order to live so that you are free to eat and free to enjoy your body, you must possess a fierce sense of personal worthiness. Please don't worry if that is something you don't currently have. It is something you absolutely can acquire.

The very best strategy I know for acquiring a strong sense of personal worthiness is to surround yourself with others who have learned how. Thankfully there are many generous souls who have shared their stories to make the path smoother for the rest of us.

I want to remind you that to bring forth a good relationship with your body, there are two very distinct jobs you can choose to do. There is the personal journey of finding self-acceptance and reclaiming your body autonomy. Then there is the job of rejecting social structures that keep anti-fat bias alive and kicking.

For thin and small-to-medium fat folk, it's tempting to focus *solely* on learning to accept our bodies and reclaiming our autonomy. This group has the privilege of the world working for them in ways that the fatter among us don't. The thin and small fat people won't ever arrive in a waiting room and not fit into a chair. Or not be able to shop for clothes on the high street. Or be assumed to be lazy. Or be given diet advice when they go to the doctor for an ear infection.

To pursue self-acceptance while failing to challenge anti-fat bias means nothing will change for the next generation. Not really. That may not be important to you, but if you are serious about wanting your descendants to live in a world that respects people for who they are on the inside without prejudice due to size (or anything else), part of that means making sure it's a welcoming place for those of us who are fat.

Breaking the cycle

There is one last question I want to address before pointing you toward resources for yourself and your family. Do you have to get yourself perfectly sorted to create a space for your children to have a healthy relationship with food and feel at home in their bodies? In other words, do you have to love your own body in order to avoid passing down the habits, beliefs and unhelpful dogma that many of us learned and absorbed while growing up? No. It's not a prerequisite. But taking some steps towards your own food competence and body confidence will go a long way.

There is evidence to show that children of parents who don't smack-talk their body (or other people's bodies) and don't diet are more likely to have a good relationship with their bodies. But that doesn't mean that if you have talked badly about yourself or dieted in front of them in the past you are to blame for their struggles in the future. You know by now that our culture is soaked to the core in anti-fatness and body shaming, and those who live with people who are actively working to change those unhelpful narratives will still encounter countless messages telling them their body is wrong. Besides, there is enough parent-blame in the world without adding this too!

Resources for you

Here's what I suggest. Look for books that include the experience of people living in fat bodies and ones that suggest a way of embracing our bodies while challenging anti-fat bias. *What We Don't Talk About When We Talk About Fat* by Aubrey Gordon, *Body Respect* by Lindo Bacon and Lucy Aphramor and *Intuitive Eating* by Evelyn Tribole and Elyse Resch are great places to start.

Join Facebook groups and listen to podcasts that are based on intuitive eating, Health at Every Size (HAES), fat positivity, anti-fat bias, body acceptance and body positivity (being very careful to ensure that they are not using body positivity or intuitive eating to promise you weight loss). I suggest listening to the podcasts *Maintenance Phase, The Bod Almighty,* and *Rethinking Wellness.*

A couple of good newsletters to subscribe to are *Burnt Toast* by Virginia Sole-Smith and *Weight and Healthcare* by Ragen Chastain.

Consider coaching or taking an online course to help you break down your anti-fat bias and practice self-acceptance and care. Isabel Foxen Duke's *Stop Fighting Food* course and Michelle Yandle's *Empowered Eating* are excellent examples.

Less is more

Many parents tell me that I have changed their lives, and the lives of their children. But what does that really mean? It's taken me a while to figure out the nuance of this claim because, in truth, it's not 'me' that has changed anything. Many of these parents were suffering as they watched their child developing an out-of-control relationship with food, becoming ashamed of their bodies and heading down what seemed to be a one-way road. But that suffering has stopped.

The parents are calmer, they can trust their child and they're no longer seeing red flags. Those parents also tell me their own relationship with food and the way they feel about themselves has shifted in positive ways too.

Two things seem to happen at once to get to this new, calmer, ground-breaking way of parenting.

Firstly, the parents learn new tools, new information and new ways to apply it. They understand the misinformation that underpins many ideas about health and weight. They recognise the injustices and health risks perpetuated by this misinformation. They learn practical ways to have different conversations, set different consequences and form new expectations for their child. And yet all of that isn't where the real change happens.

Real change happens in the second part, when parents loosen up. Many say that before they heard the messages I share, they had tried many other tools, strategies and methods of parenting around food and behaviours they wanted to change. They reported talking with lots of different people. They had searched online, read books and attended seminars. And while there were good aspects to what they had learned, nothing really stuck. Their children were still behaving in concerning ways around food or saying they hated how they looked, spending too much time online or refusing to sleep. Sometimes the tools and strategies they learned in these books and seminars led to them feeling more worried and wound up, not less.

Can you see how the new tools you've learned in this book will help you to loosen up? Remember, saying over and over again 'Finish your veggies' or 'You're not fat' does nothing to make a child eat more vegetables or feel good about their body, either in the moment or in the long run. In fact, it normally just adds to the stress and anxiety for both of you.

But when we simply put the veggies in the middle of the table without comment, or when we listen to and respect our kids, we can relax and remember who they are and what they are capable of. In turn, they are more likely to believe in their own capabilities and treat their bodies well.

Before becoming a writer, I was a professional artist. I travelled the world, exhibiting and selling my paintings for a living. One of the most rewarding experiences of this time was being offered advice and help from other artists. I was gifted many tips and tricks about using colour and choosing surfaces, creating compositions or themes, and finding my unique voice – all things that are important and necessary aspects of making art. But the real magic happened when I was encouraged to trust the process; when I learned to breathe calmly and hold my brushes loosely.

When we approach art by trying to make the perfect painting or trying to fix something that isn't working, we often stifle creativity. The marks we make become forced and the composition doesn't work. But when we allow ourselves to *be* with the art, allowing it to be free and to guide us, then something special happens. It's a remarkable act of trust, to make art like that. And so it is with parenting.

After finishing this book, you'll be invited again by many, many others to do *more* as a parent. Make your kids eat the 'right' foods and

When we simply put the veggies in the middle of the table without comment, or when we listen to and respect our kids, we can relax and remember who they are and what they are capable of. In turn, they are more likely to believe in their own capabilities and treat their bodies well.

get enough exercise, ensure they don't get too anxious, and prevent life from being unfair to them. You'll be encouraged to do more to protect them from the ever-growing list of harms from which a parent is supposed to protect their child.

But sometimes to achieve all this, we need to do *less*. Less, if it's harm they can figure out how to manage themselves, or if behind our actions is the belief that 'I have to fix and change you'. Less, if we're asking our child to blindly follow our lead, or if we're unconsciously attempting to take away their incredible resourcefulness, intelligence and ability. We definitely need to do less if we've forgotten to give them space to make mistakes, try again and come to us for help when they need it.

Doing less is often the hardest thing to do in this modern world of parenting. It can feel as though it flies in the face of so many deeply held beliefs.

But when we loosen up, let go and trust our child to run their own life and be their own person, it can change us and our child. It changes our need to control them. We no longer need our child to merely follow our orders. Instead, we look to control the way we respond to them and how we can change our environment. When this happens, our child's need to change their body decreases. Their fight with food dissipates. They no longer look for significance or belonging in external factors. They no longer seek agency over us because they have plenty of agency over themselves.

This book is your first step in implementing this new way of parenting. Make the very best use of it you can and lend it to anyone who might need it. I wish you all the very best.

ACKNOWLEDGEMENTS

Writing any book requires many quiet hours alone, but few books are a solitary endeavour. Indeed, there are numerous hands and hearts behind the pages of this one. As I reflect on my journey, I am touched by gratitude for those who stood by me, supported me and contributed in big and small ways.

First, I want to acknowledge Abby, my editor. To say that this book would not exist without her is no exaggeration. The initial idea of the book was hers. Not only did her peerless editorial wisdom make me a better writer, but her friendship went beyond. Through revisions and challenging decisions, her smarts and wordsmithing skills helped bring my thoughts into a coherent, readable narrative.

A special acknowledgement must also go to Christine, my book coach. With every session, every critique and every word of encouragement, she shaped and steered this book. I am thankful for the confidence and clarity she instilled in me.

To the publishing team at HarperCollins: Alex, Holly, Madeleine and Sandra; thank you. From the initial pitch to the final print, your efforts to ensure its success have been evident. I love being in the company of such a committed and passionate team.

To my fellow authors and friends from the literary world: your invaluable advice at the start of this project has been appreciated and acted on. It would have been a different book if not for your generosity.

To those who supported me via Patreon: thank you for your belief in this book. The difference it has made is immeasurable.

To the supporters of my first book, made possible by your Kickstarter contributions: I can't acknowledge your support enough.

To my friends: your patience, coffee dates and willingness to listen to rambles and rants about the writing process have kept me on solid ground. I owe you.

To the generous parents who agreed to have their stories included in this book: thank you again. Without you, this book would be very different. I hope you know the importance of your contribution.

And to my family both immediate and wide: I couldn't have done it without your love. Nothing is more important or more valued. Thank you.

REFERENCES AND ENDNOTES

For a full list of the reference material consulted in the writing of this book, visit: emmawright.co.nz/book-references.

Introduction

we have almost 100 years of research on this topic: Ragen Chastain, *Weight and Healthcare,* Substack newsletter; weightandhealthcare.substack.com/

If 'not being fat' plays a large role in the body confidence we teach: T. L. Tylka and J. A. Wilcox, 'Are intuitive eating and healthy eating compatible? Intuitive eating dissociates eating behaviors from weight control outcomes and its influence is mediated by autonomous motivation', *Journal of Behavioral Medicine*, 2020, vol.43, no.1, pp.131–142.

There is research to suggest that children can become relaxed around food: Ellyn Satter, *Child of Mine: Feeding with Love and Good Sense,* Bull Publishing Company, 2001.

programmes that include a weight loss goal (either explicit or implied): Joshua Wolrich, *Food Isn't Medicine,* Ebury Publishing, Kindle Edition, 2021.

Those things tend to work against our long-term health: Lindo Bacon and Lucy Aphramor, *Body Respect: What Conventional Health Books Get Wrong, Leave Out, and Just Plain Fail to Understand About Weight,* BenBella Books, 2014.

SECTION ONE: FOOD

Chapter 1

a child who has their diet largely controlled by their parents: Ellyn Satter, *Child of Mine,* op. cit.

many nutritionists argue that getting enough trumps all: E. Tribole and E. Resch, *Intuitive Eating: A Revolutionary Program That Works,* 4th edition, St. Martin's Essentials, 2020.

Not getting enough is uncomfortable, it makes us fixate on food: American Council on Science and Health, 2 December 2021, www.acsh.org/news/2021/12/02/can-you-be-addicted-food-probably-not-15968; and Virginia Sole-Smith, 'Is Sugar Really Addictive?', *Burnt Toast*, audio podcast and Substack newsletter, 25 August 2022, virginiasolesmith.substack.com/p/is-sugar-really-addictive#details

Kids stop sneaking food and fixating on it; they are calmer: Ellyn Satter, 'Eating competence: Definition and evidence for the Satter Eating Competence Model', *Journal of Nutrition Education and Behavior,* 2007, vol.39, no.2, pp.142–153.

Emotional eating … is by and large a natural and healthy aspect of eating: Isabel Foxen Duke, Stop Fighting Food website, stopfightingfood.com

Chapter 2

She asks us to imagine that our children walk around: Amy McCready, Positive Parenting Solutions website, www.positiveparentingsolutions.com/parenting/what-is-positive-parenting

In his book Lost Connections, *Johann Hari points:* Johann Hari, *Lost Connections: Why You're Depressed and How to Find Hope,* Bloomsbury, 2019.

Some parenting experts suggest we should seldom do something for a child: Amy McCready, *Me, Me, Me Epidemic: A Step-By-Step Guide*

To Raising Capable, Grateful Kids In An Over-Entitled World, Tarcher, 2016.

kids spell love 'T.I.M.E.' so when you give your kids Power Time they will experience being loved: 'Love: Children Spell Love T.I.M.E.', www.imom.com/love-children-spell-love-t-i-m-e

Chapter 3

eating competence leads to better health outcomes in later life: Ellyn Satter, 'Giving children autonomy with eating: What it *is*—and *isn't*': Ellyn Satter Institute, 2021, www.ellynsatterinstitute.org/family-meals-focus-no-110-giving-children-autonomy-with-eating/

Ellyn Satter suggests dividing the responsibilities within the feeding relationship between you and your child: Ellyn Satter, *Secrets of Feeding a Healthy Family: How to Eat, How to Raise Good Eaters, How to Cook*, Kelcy Press, 2005.

linking foods to body size adds to weight stigma and anxiety: Gemma Tatangelo, Marita McCabe, David Mellor and Alex Mealey, 'A Systematic Review of Body Dissatisfaction and Sociocultural Messages Related to the Body among Preschool Children', *Body Image*, 18 September 2016, pp.86–95.

Evans argues that it's not possible to be addicted to something the human body needs: Marci Evans, 'Sugar Addiction: A Summary of the Science', Marci RD Nutrition website, 3 February 2018, marcird.com/sugar-addiction-summary-science/

Carbohydrates are the only fuel the brain can use to function: Scott Edwards, 'Sugar and the Brain', *Harvard Medical School*, 2016, hms.harvard.edu/news-events/publications-archive/brain/sugar-brain

there are no potentially harmful side effects of 'coming off' refined sugar: Marci Evans, 'Sugar Addiction: A Summary of the Science', op. cit.

Dr Joshua Wolrich in his book Food Isn't Medicine *gives a great explanation*: Joshua Wolrich, *Food Isn't Medicine*, op. cit.

Chapter 4

The Centers for Disease Control and Prevention (CDC) in the United States: 'Social Determinants of Health at CDC', Centers for Disease Control and Prevention, 2022, www.cdc.gov/socialdeterminants/FAQ.html.

In their book Body Respect, *Lindo Bacon and Lucy Aphramor show that:* Lindo Bacon and L Aphramor, *Body Respect,* op. cit.

research suggests praise can have the opposite effect: A. Kohn, *Punished by Rewards: The Trouble with Gold Stars, Incentive Plans, A's, Praise, and Other Bribes,* Houghton Mifflin, 1993.

Carol Dweck ... conducted a series of studies on 412 ten- to twelve-year-old school students in New York: C. S. Dweck and C. M. Mueller, 'Praise for intelligence can undermine children's motivation and performance', *Journal of Personality and Social Psychology,* 1998, vol.75, no.1, pp.33–52.

the study by Lepper and Greene that followed preschool children who showed artistic talent: M.R. Lepper and D. Greene, 'Effects of extrinsic reward on children's intrinsic motivation', *Child Development* 1974, 45, pp.1141–1145, bingschool.stanford.edu/sites/bingschool/files/1974_greenelepper.pdf

Alfie Kohn ... backs up this research by showing that kids who are raised on rewards: A. Kohn, *Punished by Rewards,* op. cit.

SECTION TWO: FAT

Chapter 5

American life insurance companies began to create their own height and weight tables: A. Gordon and M. Hobbs, 'The Body Mass Index', *Maintenance Phase,* audio podcast, 3 August 2021, podcasts.apple.com/nz/podcast/the-body-mass-index/id1535408667?i=1000530850955

Some charts differed by as much as 18 kilos: Ibid.

'ethically repugnant': G. Eknoyan, 'Adolphe Quetelet (1796-1874) – The Average Man and Indices of Obesity', *Nephrology Dialysis Transplantation,* 2008, vol.23, no.1, pp.47–51.

we simply didn't have data to prove childhood BMI would determine health problems: Aubrey Gordon, *You Just Need to Lose Weight and 19 Other Myths About Fat People,* Beacon Press, 2023.

When the World Health Organization made these decisions: World Health Organization, 'Obesity and overweight', fact sheet, 9 June 2021, www.who.int/news-room/fact-sheets/detail/obesity-and-overweight

Millions of Americans became 'fat', Wednesday – even if they didn't gain a pound: 'Who's fat? New definition adopted', CNN, 17 June 1998, edition.cnn.com/HEALTH/9806/17/weight.guidelines/

'obesity epidemic' research is conducted from a starting position of 'knowing' fat is bad: D. Gallagher, S. B. Heymsfield, M. Heo, S. A. Jebb, P. R. Murgatroyd, and Y. Sakamoto, 'Healthy percentage body fat ranges: An approach for developing guidelines based on body mass index', *The American Journal of Clinical Nutrition*, 2000, vol.72, no.3, pp.694–701.

Chapter 6

Underweight BMI is correlated with early death: Ragen Chastain, *Weight and Healthcare,* op. cit.

Ragen Chastain ... asks us to imagine what would happen: Ibid.

it is notoriously difficult to reverse public opinion once it has been formed: Timothy Caulfield, *Is Gwyneth Paltrow Wrong About Everything?: When Celebrity Culture and Science Clash*, Beacon Press, 2018.

There are several limitations to self-reported data when it comes to weight and nutrition studies: Ragen Chastain, *Weight and Healthcare,* op. cit.

A study with fewer than 600 participants does not provide statistically meaningful results: Ben Goldacre, *Bad Science: Quacks, Hacks and Big Pharma Flacks,* HarperCollins, 2009.

Weight-loss studies must be conducted over at least five years: Ragen Chastain, *Weight and Healthcare,* op. cit.

Chapter 7

By age 45, the average British woman has embarked on 61 diets: 'Women have tried 61 diets by age of 45', *New Zealand Herald,* 20 March 2012.

1 in 210 if you are a man and 1 in 124 if you are a woman: A. Fildes, J. Charlton, C. Rudisill, P. Littlejohns, A. T. Prevost and M. C. Gulliford, 'Probability of an obese person attaining normal body weight: Cohort study using electronic health records', *American Journal of Public Health,* 2015, vol.105, no.9, pp.54–59.

after three to five years, 95–98% of dieters will regain all the weight they lost: Ibid.

the people who are most likely to succeed on a diet (the 2–5%): Ibid.

People who attempt to lose weight and fail are generally not lazy: Aubrey Gordon, *You Just Need to Lose Weight and 19 Other Myths About Fat People,* op. cit.

only 2–5% of people achieve lasting long-term weight loss: L. Bacon and L. Aphramor. 'Weight science: Evaluating the evidence for a paradigm shift', *Nutrition Journal,* 2011, vol.10, no.1, pp.1–13.

collectively, we get fatter every year: World Health Organization, 'Obesity and overweight', op. cit.

Here's what happens when 100 11-year-olds are put on a diet: Cynthia Bulik, 'Dr Cynthia Bulik, Eating disorders: replacing myths with realities', YouTube, 22 April 2015.

although some argue this weight is only kept off via disordered eating practices: D. Burgard, 'What is "Health at Every Size"?' in *The Fat Studies Reader,* edited by E. Rothblum and S. Solovay, New York University Press, 2009.

Weight loss gets harder and harder to achieve the more often you attempt it: Lindo Bacon and Lucy Aphramor, *Body Respect,* op. cit.

a long-term dieter is more likely to end up with an eating disorder than sustained weight loss: Ibid.

45 million Americans go on a diet each year: L. Searing, 'The Big Number: 45 million Americans go on a diet each year', *Washington Post,* 1 January 2018.

9% of Americans will get an eating disorder in their lifetime: ANAD (National Association of Anorexia Nervosa and Associated Disorders), 'Eating Disorder Statistics', anad.org/education-and-awareness/about-eating-disorders/eating-disorders-statistics

In New Zealand it is conservatively estimated that 4% of our population live with an eating disorder: Eating Disorders Victoria, 'Eating Disorders Key Research and Statistics', www.eatingdisorders.org.au/eating-disorders-a-z/eating-disorder-statistics-and-key-research

genetics account for somewhere between 40% and 60% of one's likelihood of developing an eating disorder: C. M. Bulik, J. R. Coleman, J. A. Hardaway, L. Breithaupt, H. J. Watson, C. D. Bryant and G. Breen, 'Genetics and neurobiology of eating disorders', *Nature Neuroscience*, 2022 May, vol.25, no.5, pp.543-54.

every measure of human size increased at the same time, so that we became taller as well as fatter: Lindo Bacon and Lucy Aphramor, *Body Respect*, op. cit.

a New Zealand documentary about a weight loss study in which fat teenagers ate the poop of thin teenagers: *The Good Sh*t*, TV Three, documentary series, 2018. (A New Zealand documentary series which explores the potential of using faecal microbiota transplantation [FMT] as a weight-loss method.)

fatter kids in general eat fewer calories than thinner ones: Ellyn Satter, *Child of Mine*, op. cit.

there are over 100 factors that contribute to someone's size: Joshua Wolrich, *Food Isn't Medicine*, op. cit.

Chapter 8

the cost to the country outstrips the revenue it brings in by $6.657 billion: B. Easton, 'The Social Costs of Alcohol: A New Zealand Study', The Social Policy Evaluation and Research Unit, 2014.

fat folks are paid less and are underrepresented in management positions: E. Han, E. C. Norton and S. C. Stearns, 'Weight and wages: fat versus lean paychecks', *Health Economics*, 2009, vol.18, no.5, pp.535–548.

If a fatter person goes with the same complaint: Aubrey Gordon, *What We Don't Talk About When We Talk About Fat*, Beacon Press, 2021.

our collective health would increase if our systems stopped stigmatising fat people: A. Brown, S. W. Flint and R.L. Batterham, 'Pervasiveness, impact and implications of weight stigma', EClinicalMedicine, May 2022, vol.1, p.47.

Fatter people are more likely to put off going to the doctor: Ragen Chastain, *Weight and Healthcare*, op. cit.

kids as young as three already believe that fat is bad and thin is good: Virginia Sole-Smith, *Fat Talk: Parenting in the Age of Diet Culture*, Henry Holt and Company, 2023.

In a 2021 UK court case, two teenagers were removed from loving parents: Nadeem Badshah and agency, 'Two Teenagers Placed in Foster Care After Weight Loss Plan Fails' *The Guardian*, 11 March 2021.

the only form of cultural stigma that has grown significantly in the last 20 years is anti-fat bias: Tessa E. S. Charlesworth and Mahzarin R. Banaji, 'Research: How Americans' Biases Are Changing (or Not) Over Time', *Harvard Business Review*, 2 August 2019, hbr.org/2019/08/research-on-many-issues-americans-biases-are-decreasing

The argument against fatness back then was that it was associated too closely with Black people: Sabrina Strings, *Fearing the Black Body: The Racial Origins of Fat Phobia*, New York University Press, 2019.

In schools, size bullying is the most common form of bullying: Aubrey Gordon, *What We Don't Talk About When We Talk About Fat*, op. cit.

four out of five teenage girls think sport is hard to participate in: Anna Beard, 'Why Should We Still Care About Body Image?' YWCA, 2 December 2020, www.ywca.org.nz/our-stories/how-do-young-women-in-aotearoa-feel-about-their-bodies

A survey conducted by Glamour magazine said that 97% of women: Shaun Dreisbach, 'Shocking Body-Image News: 97% of Women Will Be Cruel to Their Bodies Today', *Glamour*, 2 February 2011, www.glamour.com/story/shocking-body-image-news-97-percent-of-women-will-be-cruel-to-their-bodies-today

The global business of weight loss as part of the wellness industry is valued around $USD1.5 trillion: S. Callaghan, M. Lösch, A. Pione and W. Teichner, 'Feeling good: The future of the $1.5 trillion wellness market', *McKinsey & Company*, 8 April 2021, www.mckinsey.com/industries/consumer-packaged-goods/our-insights/feeling-good-the-future-of-the-1-5-trillion-wellness-market

Coming out as gay isn't about being willing to tell the world you're homosexual: A. Gordon and M. Hobbs, 'The Body Mass Index', *Maintenance Phase*, op. cit.

Chapter 9

eliminating anti-fat messages from your environment: Marcia Evans, Marci RD Nutrition website, marcird.com

menopausal women are the second largest at-risk group of developing an eating disorder after teenage girls: J. H. Baker and C. D. Runfola, 'Eating disorders in midlife women: A perimenopausal eating disorder?' *Maturitas*, 2016, vol.85, pp.112–116.

why would kids as young as three ... believe that fatness is so bad?: P. Cramer and T. Steinwert, 'Thin is good, fat is bad: How early does it begin?', *Journal of Applied Developmental Psychology*, 1998, vol.19, no.3, pp.429–451.

Practising gratitude has been shown to make us feel calmer: Johann Hari, *Lost Connections: Uncovering the Real Causes of Depression – and the Unexpected Solutions*, Bloomsbury Publishing, 2018.

embracing the size they are can lead to better long-term health outcomes: Ragen Chastain, *Weight and Healthcare*, op. cit.

SECTION THREE: FEAR

Chapter 10

It's a game-changing structure adapted from an approach: Michelle Icard, *Fourteen Talks by Age Fourteen*, Penguin Random House, 2023.

Chapter 11

defines binge eating disorder as a 'serious, life-threatening, yet treatable eating disorder': National Eating Disorders Association (USA), www.nationaleatingdisorders.org

Corissa Enneking's story, told by Michael Hobbs in The Huffington Post, *is a good example*: Michael Hobbs, 'Everything you Know About Obesity Is Wrong', *The Huffington* Post, 19 September 2018, highline.huffingtonpost.com/articles/en/everything-you-know-about-obesity-is-wrong

Chapter 12

kids who are told 'not to' by parents are more likely to experiment with that very thing: K. F. Stanger-Hall and D. W. Hall, 'Abstinence-only education and teen pregnancy rates: Why we need comprehensive sex education in the U.S.' *PLoS One*, 2011, vol.6, no.10, published online.

Many kids will have seen porn by the time they are eight: Philippa Wain, 'Children's Commissioner: Pornography affecting 8-year-olds' behaviour', *BBC News,* 9 May 2023, www.bbc.com/news/technology-65534354

You've already asked me that and I've given my answer: Amy McCready, Positive Parenting Solutions blog, www.positiveparentingsolutions.com/parenting-blog

Chapter 13

symptoms of sleep deprivation can be similar to those of ADHD: J. A. Owens, 'The ADHD and sleep conundrum: a review', *Journal of Developmental & Behavioral Pediatrics,* 2005, vol.26, no.4, pp.312–322.

A healthy child will not regularly snore or make excessive noise in sleeping: E. Suni and J. Gould, 'Snoring in Children', *The Sleep Foundation,* updated 14 August 2023, www.sleepfoundation.org/snoring/snoring-children

Chapter 14

Michelle Icard suggests approaching devices with the same caution: Michelle Icard, *Fourteen Talks by Age Fourteen,* op. cit.

The contract is loosely based on a tech contract designed by Amy McCready from Positive Parenting Solutions: Natalie Tysdal, 'Helping Families Set Boundaries With Technology with Amy McCready, Positive Parenting Solutions', *The Natalie Tysdal Podcast,* 11 January 2022, www.youtube.com/watch?v=vP2A_YdOpKc

Online bullying … is one of the leading factors when it comes to teen suicide: A. Schonfeld, D. McNiel, T. Toyoshima and R. Binder, 'Cyberbullying and adolescent suicide', *Journal of the American Academy of Psychiatry and the Law Online*, February 2023.

RESOURCES AND HELPFUL LINKS

These are a starting point for finding resources to help your child. Additional resources can be found at: emmawright.co.nz/book-resources

Please check that resource details are current before passing them on to your child or your friends.

Eating disorders

Eating Disorders Association of NZ – practical information: 0800 2 EDANZ (0800 2 33269), www.ed.org.nz

Eating Disorders Carer Support NZ – provides support and extensive resources: admin@edcs.co.nz, www.facebook.com/EDCSNZ/

Recovered Living NZ – information about recovery and inhouse programs: recoveredlivingnz.com

The Butterfly Foundation – good information in Australia: 1800 33 4673, butterfly.org.au

US National Eating Disorder Association (NEDA) – lots of good resources and information: www.nationaleatingdisorders.org

ANAD (National Association of Anorexia Nervosa and Associated Disorders) – support, connection and community; provides good resources and information: anad.org

Resource for selective or picky eaters

Judith Yeabsley, 'The Confident Eater': theconfidenteater.com

Weight-inclusive nutrition services including picky eating

'Dietitian at your table': www.dietitianatyourtable.nz

Nicole Cruz – US based, international focused: nicolecruzrd.com

'The Food Tree': www.thefoodtree.co

Interview with Evelyn Tribole

emmawright.co.nz/evelyn-tribole-intuitive-eating

Body-inclusive books for toddlers to teens

For tweens/teens: www.splitrockbks.com/burnt-toast-middle-grade-young-adult

For littlies: www.splitrockbks.com/burnt-toast-picture-books

For some extra ideas: emmawright.co.nz/body-positive-books

Bedtime gratitude script

For kids up to age nine: emmawright.co.nz/wp-content/uploads/2023/08/BEDTIME-GRATITUDE.pdf

Talking to youth about porn

Keep it real: keepitrealonline.govt.nz/parents/pornography

The Light Project: thelightproject.co.nz

Netsafe: netsafe.org.nz/advice/parenting

Healthy Online Engagement Contract

Downloadable contract template: emmawright.co.nz/wp-content/uploads/2023/10/Healthy-Online-Engagement-Contract.pdf

Helplines NZ

Parent Helpline: 0800 568 856

Youthline – 12- to 26-year-olds and their families via phone, text, email or face-to-face (in some regions): 0800 376 633, free text 234, talk@youthline.co.nz

What's Up? – 5- to 19-year-olds via phone or webchat with trained counsellors: 0800 942 8787, www.whatsup.co.nz

Helplines Australia

Kids Helpline – 5- to 25-year-olds via webchat, phone or email: 1800 55 1800, kidshelpline.com.au

Headspace – 12- to 25-year-olds and families via phone or online: 1800 650 890, headspace.org.au/online-and-phone-support

Other helpful resources

NZ Mental Health Foundation Resources: mentalhealth.org.nz/resources

National Youth Mental Health Foundation – 12- to 25-year-olds: headspace.org.au

Resources for Māori and Pasifika

www.auntydee.co.nz

www.thelowdown.co.nz

Gender and sexuality

NZ helpline: OutLine – LGBTIQA+/Rainbow, 0800 688 5463

NZ service: RainbowYOUTH – ry.org.nz

NZ resource: Be There – be-there.nz

Australian resource: Families Like Mine – www.beyondblue.org.au/who-does-it-affect/lesbian-gay-bi-trans-and-intersex-lgbti-people/families-like-mine